John Godber
Plays: 2

Teechers, Happy Jack, September in the Rain, Salt of the Earth

Teechers: 'Taps powerfully into everybody's inherited nostalgia, anger and concern about what school did to them, failed to do for them, or is in the process of wasting on their behalf.' *Guardian*
'Written and played with realism, thumbnail observation and narrative drive.' *The Times*

Happy Jack: 'The subjects are his grandparents . . . The play works backwards through the marriage . . . It is all snappily and often hilariously done . . . Neat, touching and joyously celebratory.' *Financial Times*
'Transmitted with a directness that touches the heart.' *Guardian*

September in the Rain: 'A little gem. Godber's great compassion for his characters and his rare gift for dialogue make for a poignant study of two real flesh and blood people, stumbling through the foolish rows and inarticulate frustrations of an ordinary marriage . . . The play is powered by the rough dry wit of Yorkshire, and tinged with a gentle nostalgia for a time when folk were folk and nowt were queer as that.' *Scotsman*

Salt of the Earth: 'It's the tension between the rigid security of closed working-class communities in the fifties and their opening up to new influences – some more reet than others – that the show explores . . . Why aren't there more like this?' *Guardian*
'A heartwarming, richly human yarn right out of everyday life and the quixotic dreams of a lifetime . . . Like any honest autobiographical work, it is bitingly funny, recognisably true in its details and flooded with the pains, joys, and disappointments and triumphs of ordinary living . . . Sturdily real moment by moment, it is grand, sweeping and memorable by its finish.' *Chicago Tribune*

John Godber was born in Upton, near Pontefract, in 1956. He trained as a teacher at Bretton Hall College, Wakefield, did an MA in Drama and an MPhil/PhD in Drama at Leeds University. Since 1984 he has been Artistic Director of Hull Truck Theatre Company. His plays include: *Happy Jack*, *September in the Rain*, *Bouncers* (winner of seven Los Angeles Critics Circle awards), *Up 'n' Under* (Olivier Comedy of the Year Award, 1984), *Shakers* and *Shakers Restirred* (both with Jane Thornton), *Up 'n' Under 2*, *Blood, Sweat and Tears*, *Teechers*, *Salt of the Earth*, *On the Piste*, *Happy Families* (commissioned by British Telecom for the Little Theatre Guild of Great Britain and premiered by 49 amateur companies on the same night in 1991, the biggest ever theatrical opening), *The Office Party*, *April in Paris*, *Passion Killers* and *Lucky Sods*. Television and film work includes: *The Ritz*, *The Continental*, *My Kingdom for a Horse*, *Chalkface* (all BBC2), episodes of *Crown Court*, *Grange Hill* and *Brookside* and screenplays for *On the Piste* and *Up 'n' Under*. He is an honorary lecturer at Bretton Hall College and a DLitt. of Hull University.

* published by Methuen

JOHN GODBER

Plays: 2

Teechers
Happy Jack
September in the Rain
Salt of the Earth

introduced by the author

Methuen Drama

METHUEN CONTEMPORARY DRAMATISTS

1 3 5 7 9 10 8 6 4 2

This collection first published in the United Kingdom in 2001 by
Methuen Publishing Limited
215 Vauxhall Bridge Road, London SW1V 1EJ

Teechers was first published in the United Kingdom in 1989 by Samuel French Ltd
Copyright © 1989 by John Godber
Happy Jack was first published in the United Kingdom in 1989 by Penguin Books Ltd
Copyright © 1989 by John Godber
September in the Rain was first published in the United Kingdom in 1989 by
Penguin Books Ltd
Copyright © 1989 by John Godber
Salt of the Earth was first published in the United Kingdom in 1989
by Samuel French Ltd
Copyright © 1989 by John Godber

Collection and introduction copyright © 2001 by John Godber

The right of the author to be identified as the author of these works has been asserted
by him in accordance with the Copyright, Designs and Patents Act, 1988

Methuen Publishing Limited Reg. No. 3543167

A CIP catalogue record for this book is available from the British Library

ISBN 0 413 75820 6

'I Remember It Well': words by Alan Jay Lerner, music by Frederick Loewe
© 1957 Chappell & Co. Inc., USA. Warner/Chappell Music Ltd, London W6 8BS
Lyrics reproduced by permission of IMP Ltd
'September Song': words by Maxwell Anderson, music by Kurt Weill
© 1938 Chappell & Co. Inc. and Kurt Weill Foundation For Music Inc., USA
Warner/Chappell Music Ltd, London W6 8BS
Lyrics reproduced by permission of IMP Ltd
'Little Things Mean A Lot': words and music by Edith Lindeman and Carl Stutz
© 1954 EMI Catalogue Partnership and EMI Feist Catalog Inc., USA
Worldwide print rights controlled by Warner Bros Publications Inc./IMP Ltd
Lyrics reproduced by permission of IMP Ltd
'September in the Rain' words by Al Dubin and music by Harry Warren
© 1937 Remick Music Corporation, USA
Reproduced by permission of B. Feldman & Co. Ltd, London WC2H 0QY

In addition to the licence to perform the plays, producers are required to advise the
Performing Rights Society (29–33 Berners Street, London W1, Theatres Department)
of details of performances in order that the copyright owners of the extracts of the
songs may receive their performance fees.

Typeset by Deltatype Ltd, Birkenhead, Merseyside
Printed and bound in Great Britain by Cox & Wyman Ltd, Reading, Berks

Contents

A Chronology
of first performances

Bouncers (Edinburgh Festival; Hull Truck Theatre
  Company, Donmar Warehouse, 1984)   1977
Cry Wolf (Yorkshire Actors Company)   1981
Cramp (Edinburgh Festival; then Bloomsbury 1987)   1981
EPA (Minsthorpe High School)   1982
Young Hearts Run Free (Bretton Hall)   1983
A Christmas Carol (Hull Truck)   1984
September in the Rain (Hull Truck)   1984
Up 'n' Under 1 (Hull Truck, Edinburgh Festival;
  then Donmar Warehouse)   1984
Shakers (with Jane Thornton. Hull Truck)   1984
Happy Jack (Hull Truck)   1985
Up 'n' Under 2 (Hull Truck)   1985
Cramp (musical. Hull Truck)   1986
Blood, Sweat and Tears (Hull Truck; then Tricycle
  Theatre)   1986
Oliver Twist (Hull Truck)   1987
Teechers (Hull Truck, Edinburgh Festival; Arts
  Theatre, 1988)   1987
Salt of the Earth (Wakefield Centenary; then
  Hull Truck, Edinburgh Festival; then Donmar
  Warehouse)   1988
Office Party (Nottingham Playhouse)   1989
On the Piste (Hull Truck, Derby Playhouse;
  Garrick, 1993)   1990
Everyday Heroes (with Jane Thornton. Community
  play, Bassetlaw)   1991
Bouncers, 1990s Re-mix (Hull Truck)   1991
Shakers Re-stirred (with Jane Thornton. Hull
  Truck)   1991
Happy Families (Little Theatre Guild, West
  Yorkshire Playhouse, 1992)   1991
April in Paris (Hull Truck; Ambassadors, 1994)   1992
Passion Killers (Hull Truck, Derby Playhouse)   1994

Lucky Sods (Hull Truck; then Hampstead Theatre)   1995
Dracula (with Jane Thornton. Hull Truck)   1995
Gym and Tonic (Hull Truck, Derby Playhouse)   1996
Weekend Breaks (Hull Truck, Alhambra, Bradford)   1997
It Started with a Kiss (Hull Truck)   1997
Unleashed (Hull Truck, Edinburgh Festival;
  Bloomsbury, 1999)   1998
Hooray for Hollywood (Hull Truck)   1998
Perfect Pitch (Stephen Joseph Theatre,
  Scarborough)   1998
Big Trouble in the Little Bedroom (Hull Truck)   1999
Seasons in the Sun (Hull Truck, West Yorkshire
  Playhouse)   2000
Thick as a Brick (Hull Truck)   2000

*We gratefully acknowledge the help of John Bennett and
Liverpool Hope University College in the preparation of this
chronology. Further information can be found on
www.johngodber.co.uk.*

Introduction

The plays collected in this volume can all be described
as coming from an autobiographical impulse.
Thereafter they appear to split off into two distinct
strands: teaching and mining. Since I was a teacher
and come from a mining background it is easy to see
the link between my experiences and the subject matter
of the plays. It would be wrong however to consider
these plays as solely autobiographical. My experiences
are merely the starting point for the work, a point of
reference for me as the writer. After that they develop
from any number of experiences, some directly
autobiographical, others not.

Since it is fairly clear what the subject matter of
Teechers might be, let's take it first. The idea of writing
a play about education was seeded in my mind from
the early 1980s and I had in fact written one, *EPA*,
which predates *Teechers* by some eight or nine years.
EPA – the nomenclature for an Educational Priority
Area – was a play written from 'inside' the
comprehensive system. In a way, though I didn't realise
it at the time, *EPA* was a very good template for
Teechers. It was full of bile and confused rhetoric, it was
also written by a drama teacher, who was frustrated
and angry about the state of the education system.
Though I didn't realise it, this proved not to be the
best standpoint to write from.

In fact it wasn't until *Teechers* had had some success
at the Arts Theatre in London that I realised how
close I had been to the earlier play and how much I
needed time away from my six years' teaching in order
to synthesise the experience. *EPA* was so full of rancour
and bile and a desire to get out of teaching that it had
hardly any sense of humour. Several years later when I
wrote *Teechers* I had already had some success as a
professional writer and had left teaching behind me. I

had also shaken off the bile and was able to revisit the topic with a clarity of thought and able to see the experience for what it was.

The stylistic notion behind *Teechers* was a return to basics. I based the setting of the play around the props and facilities I had had at my disposal as a drama teacher; a few chairs and desks and a whole load of imagination. *Teechers* can be performed by three actors or by sixteen actors, the parts can be 'doubled' or shared. I wanted to make the piece as flexible as possible in order to give flight to the actors' and audiences' imagination. Obviously the power of language to create atmosphere and character, to establish time and place, is absolutely crucial in this style of work. Once again I embarked on a theatrical game. The actors are kids playing teachers; there is an implicit theatrical duality which adds to what J.B. Priestley called 'the dramatic experience'. It is a convention similar to the one employed in *Bouncers*.

When directing *Teechers* I often say that if you let the plates fall the audience are left watching three actors and three chairs, but if you keep the plates spinning the audience never see three chairs and three actors, they see a huge comprehensive school at work. It is a shared experience and a piece of theatrical magic.

On a number of occasions, especially in the early eighties, I was asked whether or not I wrote political plays. I certainly didn't write the same kind of political plays as Davids Edgar or Hare. It often struck me that if a person had to ask whether or not I wrote political plays, then maybe they had not seen the play in question or deduced in some way that I didn't write political plays. Looking back on that time, I still stand by my stock answer: I did write political plays, in that any play is a view on the world and most plays are political in some small way, and given my background and upbringing how could I not have a leftist leaning?

What seemed to worry commentators was the fact

that my plays were comedies, but I hoped I wrote
comedy with bite and a point! As time has gone by
and I stand looking at the way my work has
progressed, some of the plays perhaps have more in
common with Dario Fo than I could have ever
imagined. Quite a number of the plays could be seen
as satires on our social system and especially social
injustice.

This question of political writing brings us neatly to
the three plays which feature mining as a backdrop.
For no other reason than a statement of fact, I have to
mention here that my father was made redundant after
the miners' strike. A number of friends and theatre
journalists suggested at the time that I should write a
play about the event, but it didn't seem the right thing
for me to do. In a way the event overshadowed the
people. I was too caught up in living the consequences
to be able to write about it directly. Perhaps I had
learnt through my experience with teaching that for me
a play had to 'settle inside' before you could make it a
valuable piece of theatrical literature.

In my trilogy of mining plays the people and the job
of mining are impossible to separate; one informs and
shapes the other. In 1981 I wrote *Happy Jack*, a
memory play, which uses reverse chronology to
examine the relationship of Jack and Liz. Jack is a
strong silent miner, Liz, his effusive wife. For this play
I drew on three generations of my family, my gran
and grandad, my mum and dad, and myself and my
then girlfriend, to form the relationship. I was told
later that there are many things in this play that a
writer in his early twenties ought not to know about!

Although much of *Happy Jack* is humorous, almost
everything that is said, and certainly the melting pot of
the relationship, is fed from a political source. What
makes Jack what he is the job that he does. What
makes Liz worry about Jack, and the source of her
growing neurosis, is Jack's job as a miner. There is

something absolutely intertwined in the occupation of this miner and his behaviour.

The characters Jack and Liz enjoy another outing in my favourite play, *September in the Rain*. *September in the Rain* is a gentle lyrical comedy, with what at first glance appears to be an innocent and rather sentimental story: a couple look back at their holiday times together in Blackpool. However if we peel back the surface ever so slightly and ask even the most rudimentary questions, it becomes clear that this play is fuelled by a knowledge of the mining industry and the effect it has on the individuals within its direct reference.

Even the title is loaded with irony. While also being a popular song, it refers to September week, or Leger week, from the famous horse-race at Doncaster. This was a major holiday for Yorkshire miners. My family went to Blackpool for a full week every September for the first twenty-three years of their married life. For the first twenty years of my life my holidays took place in Mavis's bed-and-breakfast down Woodfield Road. Invariably it rained and we spent a wet week doing very little! Even as a young boy the irony of miners holidaying in the rain wasn't lost on me. It was a cruel stroke of fate for men who had spent all their lives underground to go away on holiday only to be rained on!

In *Salt of the Earth* I took a more panoramic view of the rise and fall of the mining industry. Although the move from nationalisation to the miners' strike and beyond form the backbone of the play, I was careful not to make the events seem arid to the viewer. The characters and their lives had to be affected by circumstances. I felt very much that the audience would make the connections between cause and effect without me as a writer leaving signposts all over the narrative. Once again the writing in *Salt of the Earth* is funny but beneath the humour, hopefully, is the ache of humanity, of people trapped in circumstances and jobs from which they feel they cannot escape.

In brief summary then, playwriting for me starts where I am, with what I feel, how I react and try to understand in the ever-changing, fast-developing, chaotic world in which we live. An experience today might not yield a play about that experience tomorrow, or if it did it might or might not be a good play. I was told many years ago at university that all plays are about the same thing: they are about the 're-kindling of the human spirit'. I suppose that notion could be challenged but for the time being it seems as good a reason as any to keep writing!

John Godber
Hull, 2000

Teechers

a classroom comedy

Teechers was first performed by the Hull Truck Theatre Company at the Edinburgh Festival in 1987, with the following cast:

Salty (*playing* **Teacher B, Nixon, Pete Saxon, Oggy Moxon, Mr Fisher, Mr Hatton, Deanie**)   Martin Barass

Gail (*playing* **Teacher A, Ms Whitham, Oggy Moxon, Mr Basford, Miss Prime, Barry Wobschall, Dennis, Dough, Mrs Coates**)   Gill Tompkins

Hobby (*playing* **Mrs Parry, Ms Jones, Mr Basford, Ron, Piggy Patterson, Oggy Moxon, Mrs Clifton**)   Shirley Anne Selby

Directed by John Godber

Author's Note

Teechers was designed to be played by three actors, multi-role-playing twenty other parts in a play-within-a-play format. Everything about the production was reduced to the basic essentials: actors, stage, audience. I wanted to produce a play that relied on the same bare essentials that a drama teacher might have in school: kids (actors), a few chairs and desks (the set), and an audience. With these basic ingredients anything can happen in a drama lesson; indeed the characters in *Teechers* illustrate that once talent has been tapped in school the result is often staggering. Multi-role-playing is also, it must be said, an economic as well as artistic consideration. Maybe if I had twenty actors at my disposal I would have produced a different play. In this version of the play the twenty multi-roled parts have been listed in order that twenty actors (kids) could perform the play if so desired. However the play is performed, actors or students, it is important to remember that *Teechers* is a comedy, a comedy which illustrates many anxieties in education today. Comedies must primarily be funny; here is a comedy, I think, which is also deadly serious.

Act One

A comprehensive school hall. A wooden stage. There are two double desks upstage. Upstage right is an old locker with a school broom leaning against it. Downstage centre is a chair; left and right two single desks and chairs angled downstage, and three bags. A satchel, plastic bags and sports bags are near the chairs and desks. They belong to **Salty**, **Gail** *and* **Hobby** *respectively. Some music plays and* **Salty**, **Gail** *and* **Hobby** *enter, recline on the chairs and desks and look at the audience for a moment before speaking.*

Salty No more school for us so you can knackers!

Gail Salty, you nutter?

Salty What?

Gail Swearing.

Hobby Shurrup.

Salty So what?

Hobby You daft gett.

Salty It's true.

Gail Just get on with it.

Salty Nobody can do us.

Hobby We've not left yet.

Salty Knackers.

Gail Oh God he's craacked.

Hobby Shurrup.

Salty I've always wanted to be on this stage. I've always wanted to come up here and say 'knackers'. I bet you all have. Whenever I see Mrs Hudson come up on this stage to talk about litter or being a good samaritan or corn dollies or sit down first year stand

up second year I think about that word. 'Cos really
Mrs Hudson would like to come up here and say
'knackers school'. She would.

Gail Are we doing this play or what?

Salty It's like when she gets you in her office, all
neat and smelling of perfume and she says, 'You don't
come to school to fool around, Ian, to waste your time.
We treat you like young adults and we expect you to
behave accordingly. I don't think that writing on a wall
is a mature thing to do.'

Hobby That's good that, Salty, just like her.

Salty Yeh, but really she wants to say, 'Hey, Salty,
pack all this graffiti in, it's getting on my knackers.'

Gail Are we starting?

Salty Anyway why am I bothered. No more school,
no more stick, no more teachers thinking that you're
thick . . .

Gail No more of Miss Jubb shouting like you're deaf
as a post, 'Gail Saunders how dare you belch in front
of me.' Sorry, miss, didn't know it was your turn . . .

Hobby Brilliant . . .

Salty Hey, no more full school assemblies sat on the
cold floor of the sports hall freezing your knackers
off . . .

Hobby No more cross-country running, and cold
showers and towels that don't dry you.

Gail Oh and no more scenes in changing rooms
where you daren't get changed because you wear a
vest and everyone has got a bra . . .

Hobby No more Mr Thorn sending letters home
about how I missed games and was seen eating a
kebab in the Golden Spoon.

Gail   No more sweaty geog teachers with Brylcreem hush puppies.

Salty   No more trendy art teachers, who say 'Hiya' and 'Call me Gordon' . . .

Hobby   We haven't had an art teacher called Gordon.

Salty   I know.

Gail   No more having to run the fifteen hundred metres with a heart condition.

Salty   No more.

Hobby   'Cos today we're off. Twagging it for ever.

Gail   Let's start Salty.

Salty   Hang on, before we do start, we all want to thank Mr Harrison, our new drama teacher. Before he came to this school, last September, us three didn't do sod all, not a thing. He got us into this, he's a good bloke. You are, sir. I know that he's been offered a job at a better school . . . Well good luck to him . . . Before Mr Harrison came here, the teachers had given us up for dead . . . We were average.

Hobby   Lillian is average, she opens her book well, and likes a warm room.

Gail   Gail is stagnant to inert, and fights when cornered. Average.

Salty   I don't feel average today, I feel top of the class . . . thanks to sir.

Hobby   I never thought I'd be doing this, I hated drama, only took it for a doss about . . .

Salty   Right, don't forget to keep in character, and Hobby, always face the front.

Hobby   I will do.

Gail And speak up.

Hobby I will do.

Salty A lot of the stuff in the play was told to us by Mr Harrison . . .

Gail And even though you might not believe it, everything what happens in the play is based on truth.

Hobby But the names and the faces have been changed.

Salty To protect the innocent.

Gail We're going to take you to Whitewall High School. It's a comprehensive school somewhere in England . . . And they're expecting a new teacher to arrive.

Hobby There's fifteen hundred kids at Whitewall and it's a Special Priority Area which means that it's got its fair share of problems . . .

Salty All we want you to do is use your imagination because there's only three of us, and we all have to play different characters . . .

Hobby And narrators . . .

Salty And narrators.

Hobby So you'll have to concentrate . . .

Salty Oh yeh, you'll have to concentrate . . .

Gail Title . . .

Salty Oh shit, yeh . . . And it's called *Teechers*.

A sudden burst of music. They become teachers with briefcases and files, walking about a number of corridors. The lights become brighter.

Salty Morning.

Gail Morning.

Hobby   Morning.

Salty   Morning.

Hobby   Morning.

Gail   Morning.

Parry   Stop running Simon Patterson.

Teacher A   Morning, Ted.

Parry   Morning, Roy.

Teacher B   Morning, Mr Basford.

All   Morning, Mrs Parry . . .

Parry   Good morning . . .

Whitham   You are chewing, girl, spit it out. Not into her hair, into a bin . . .

Teacher B   I don't call that a straight line, do you, Claire Dickinson? No? Neither do I.

Parry   I know that was the bell, Simon Patterson. The bell is a signal for me to move and not for anyone else.

Music.

Nixon   I'm Jeff Nixon the new drama teacher. I'm looking for Mrs Parry's office.

Hobby   Up the steps in the nice part of the school, first left.

Salty *exits*.

Gail
Hobby } *(together)*   Mmmmmmmmmmm.

Gail   He doesn't look much like a teacher, he looks like somebody who's come to mend the drains.

Salty *enters as* **Nixon**.

Nixon I knew at my interview that Whitewall had a bad reputation and no drama facilities. But like a sheriff with my brand-new degree pinned to my chest I bounded up to Mrs Parry's office . . . She was busy . . . With Mr Basford the deputy head.

Gail *dons a facial mask, nose and glasses, which all the cast wear as* **Mr Basford**.

Basford I don't believe you're doing this.

Parry I run it and I shall do what I like.

Basford After all the work I've put in, now you turn around and tell me that I'm not Koko . . . Great. It's a bloody liberty.

Parry Mr Basford, I'm sorry . . . But there is nothing else to say . . . I need a younger person. I'm sure you'll have a great deal of fun in the chorus.

Basford In the chorus. I wouldn't be seen dead in the chorus.

Parry It's that or nothing, good-day, I have another appointment. Mrs Parry, or should I say Cordelia Parry, BA, M.Ed., was a huge attractive woman. She carried herself very well but had awful dress-sense, and would often mix pink with yellow. She was of large frame with a voice to match. Mr Nixon? Jeff Nixon?

Nixon That's right.

Parry Hello, nice to see you again. Coffee?

Nixon Please. Mrs Parry's office was a cavern of theatre posters . . . She certainly had more than a passing interest.

Parry Drama! Bare boards and a passion. Wonderful. This is my all-male production of *The Trojan Women*, and this is me as Ophelia.

Nixon Behind her head was a photo of a much

lither Mrs Parry in an amateur production of *Hamlet*.

Parry   I'm doing *The Mikado* in the spring term, Mr Nixon.

Nixon   I knew exactly what she meant.

Parry   I'm looking for a Koko . . .

Nixon   It must be difficult.

Parry   Mr Basford usually takes the lead in our local G and S productions but I'm afraid he was rather tiresome last year in *The Pirates* . . . We're looking for new blood . . . Well that's given you something to think about, hasn't it?

Nixon   It certainly has.

Parry   And so to business, Mr Nixon.

Nixon   The meeting went on for another twenty minutes, but I got the message. Keep any eye off for the teacher-eating girls and the thuggish boys . . . they'll have you for breakfast.

Gail   But one thing struck him about Mrs Parry. She really did care about the kids at Whitewall.

Parry   As we walked from my office, that is Mrs Parry's . . . I wished Jeff all the luck with his probationary year, and took him towards Mr Basford's room, home of the timetable. Here we are.

Nixon   The gigantic timetable was screwed to the wall. It was so colourful, so meticulous, it was a work of art, like something from the Vatican. A life's work had gone into making it.

Parry   The nomenclature is fairly straightforward. You will be NI, Mr Nixon, and drama will be DR. As you'll be having your lessons in the main hall, drama with you in the main hall, would read NIDRMH. If you have a first-year class it could read NIDRMHIYX.

Period one. Fairly simple.

Nixon   Elementary, Mrs Parry.

Parry   If you have any problems at all, Jeff, don't hesitate, come up and see me straight away, I'm always available. And don't forget about *The Mikado*. I know how much the theatre must be in your blood . . . It could be your big break . . .

Nixon   So I tentatively said yes, to a small part in the chorus, and although Mrs Parry was disappointed that I didn't want Koko, she said that I would certainly enjoy my time in Titipu.

A corridor.

Gail   Excuse me, sir?

Nixon   Eh?

Gail   Sir, I'm lost.

Nixon   Well where should you be?

Gail   Sir, I don't know, I can't work it out on my timetable. I'm in tutor group ID. But I'm in teaching group IY5 and I should be in block 43B doing biology. But 3YY6 are in there with Mr Dean doing history, he says that I should be in 31D but I've been there and the class is empty. Sir, I've been looking for my class for forty minutes.

Nixon   What have you got next?

Gail   PE in the gym.

Nixon   Do you know where that is?

Gail   Yes, sir.

Nixon   Well I suggest that you go and wait there, then at least your class'll find you.

Gail   Right, thanks sir . . .

Nixon   Oh, before you go. Have you any idea where 9IB is?

A pause. We are now in the form room.

Hobby   When you're a hardnut and fifteen you always have to give teachers a bad time. It's part of the rules of the game . . . And when there's a new teacher you can be even tougher. In our class we had seen off three tutors in as many weeks.

Gail   Miss Bell had a breakdown, but said she was pregnant.

Hobby   Then we had a supply teacher who was always crying . . .

Gail   And then they sent old Mr Willcox who was deaf so that was a laugh, we used to say anything to him.

Hobby   And now they've sent us a new teacher. A brand-new, sparkling clean, not even out of the box teacher . . .

Teacher A   They're only going to be in school for two more terms . . . Send them the new bloke Nixon . . . He can cut his teeth on 7YY down in 9IB . . . It's out of the way – if they eat him or burn him alive we can forget about him.

Salty   In 7YY there was me, Salty, Gail and Hobby who you know, Kevin Mears – who spoke funny . . . All right, Kevin?

Gail   Not bad, Salty, all right . . . I've been down to our Malcolm's, he's got a brilliant BMX. We had a great game of rally cross.

Salty   Kev was fifteen going on three. There was John Frogett who never wore any decent shoes.

Gail   Sally Wrenshaw . . .

Hobby   Vicky Marshall.

Salty   Walter Jones.

Gail   Fancy calling a kid Walter...

Salty   And Trisha Foreshore who had been through nearly all the kids in the school ... except me.

Gail   Salty, that's not true...

Salty   It is.

Gail   It is not.

Salty   Right you ask Benny Good.

Gail   I wouldn't ask Benny Good what the time was ... He's a big mouth and a liar...

Hobby   Oh come on get on with it...

Salty   And Trisha Foreshore who was known, but it might not be true, as being a bit of a goer.

Gail   That's better...

Hobby   When they sent you a new teacher, it was like getting some foster parents ... When Nixon arrived we were bored and disinterested.

Nixon   Hi ... Is this 9IB ...? I'm Mr Nixon ... It's a bit chilly in here isn't it? Can you two lads come down from the bookshelves, I don't think that they were meant for sitting on, were they? If you don't mind – just come down. And if you could stop playing table tennis that would also help. Can everybody sit on a seat and not on a desk? That's better ... Right ... My name is Mr Nixon.

Gail *and* **Hobby** *laugh.*

Nixon   The entire class burst into laughter. I didn't see that I'd said anything funny. My name is fairly straightforward and I've only got one head. I turned to the blackboard and saw that some joker had drawn

some enormous genitals on the board. I looked at the
class, they were still laughing. 'Bollocks' is not spelt
with an 'x' . . .

Hobby I don't like him.

Gail You've got to give him a chance.

Hobby Why, do you like him?

Gail No but . . . We even gave Miss Bell a chance.

Hobby He's trying to be too smart . . . I hate
teachers who call you by your nickname.

Gail Yeh, but you hate being called Lillian.
Everybody calls you Hobby.

Hobby So what, that's no reason why he should,
he's new.

*A school bell rings. Each actor goes to a desk, as kids. They
address the audience as staff.*

A number of classrooms.

Whitham Right quieten down, quieten down, said
Maureen Whitham, scale two humanities, as she
pathetically tried to control a class of thirty. Please be
quiet. If you don't keep quiet I'll have to get Mr
Basford . . . Be quiet . . . Shut up . . . Hush . . . Shhh!

Nixon As I walked through the maze of a school I
heard and saw many different types of teaching.

Whitham Please, don't throw the books about, it's
one between three, now everyone be quiet . . . BE
QUIET.

Nixon It was like a menagerie.

Hobby *becomes* **Mr Basford**.

Basford Nobody speaks in Mr Basford's lessons.
That's why I have the best maths results in the school.
Nobody talks, you can't work and talk, nobody can not

even me, and I'm a genius . . .

Nixon   Most classes had some sort of noise coming
from them . . .

Whitham   Right, said Maureen Whitham, as she
hopelessly tried to settle her class . . . I'm going to get
Mr Basford . . . Oh . . . Silence, that's better . . .

Nixon   Mr Basford's class, worked in absolute silence,
with absolute commitment. He also had the best kids.

Basford   Don't let the bastards grind you down, hit
'em low and hard . . . low and hard, kids respect
discipline . . . If they don't get it at home, they get it
in my lessons . . . Hush down . . . I can hear someone
breathing . . .

The main hall.

Nixon   I arrived at my first lesson five minutes late,
I'd taken a wrong turn at block one and found myself
in the physics block . . . A fifth-year non-exam drama
group lounged about some stacked chairs in the main
hall . . . Sixteen of them had managed to turn up.
Twenty-five names were on the register. The school
hall looked like a youth club; I walked purposefully to
the stage.

Gail   Oh God it's him, Dixon.

Hobby   Got him for tutor and for drama.

Gail   What happened to Mrs Hugill?

Hobby   Left. I hate drama. Only did it for a skive.

Gail   Yeh and me, it was this or music. Got any cigs?

Hobby   They wouldn't let me do music, said I was
too clumsy. I've got two Woodbines, my granny's.

Gail   Buy a tab off you at break?

Nixon   Get a chair, I said in a friendly, sort of youth worker type of tone.

Hobby   What's he say?

Nixon   Grab a chair everyone . . .

Gail   We're not doing any work, are we, sir?

Nixon   Can you grab a chair . . .

Gail   I'll give you some crisps if I can tab you . . .

Nixon   Can you all please get a chair and come and sit around the stage in a half-circle . . .

Hobby   How long have you been smoking?

Gail   About four months . . .

Hobby   Why don't you buy some bastard cigs then . . . ?

Gail   I am going to do.

Hobby   When?

Gail   Tomorrow . . .

Nixon   Can you get a chair and stop waving them around? I know I just said get a chair but I didn't expect you to swing it around your head . . .

Hobby   If I tab you and you don't bring any cigs I'll drop you . . .

Gail   I will, honest . . . Honest, I will . . .

Nixon   Get a chair and sit on the BASTARD . . .

Gail   What's he say?

Hobby   Dunno.

Nixon   Will everyone please sit on a chair?

Gail   Who's he think he is?

Hobby   Are you going to bio or are you twagging it?

Gail Is she here?

Hobby Her car's here. It's that red 'un.

Gail I'm off downtown then, get a milk shake.

Nixon When everyone is ready ... Good ... I think it would be a good thing for us to start with a very important person in the world of drama. Mr William Shakespeare. And in particular a play that you've probably seen but don't realise it. *Romeo and Juliet.*

Gail *and* **Hobby** *groan.*

Nixon Which is a tragedy.

Gail And it's the basis for *West Side Story*, and it's about neighbours arguing.

Hobby We've done it ...

Nixon Oh ...

Hobby We did it with Mrs Hugill.

Gail And we did about two tramps who're waiting for somebody and he never turns up.

Hobby And that was boring.

Gail And we've done *Hamlet.* About a prince who kills his uncle. Haven't we?

Hobby Yeh. And two killers who are after somebody and one of 'em's a deaf and dumb waiter.

Gail And we've done *Beverly Hills Cop. Beverly Hills Cop Two* ...

Hobby *Neighbours* ...

Gail *Eastenders* ... 'Hello, Arfur ... All right, my love.'

Hobby Good that ...

Gail What else have we done?

Hobby   *Indiana Jones.*

Gail   Yeh. *Jewel of the Nile* . . . We've done all there is
in drama . . .

Nixon   At that moment, a giant of a lad, Peter Saxon
stood up. He must hve been six feet seven, with tattoos
on his arms and a line across his neck which read 'Cut
here.' 'I wanna say something,' he said. 'I've got some
drama to tell you . . .' 'Go on then, Peter,' I said, not
knowing what to expect . . . (*He becomes* **Pete Saxon**.)
Right I'm Peter Saxon now . . . One day, sir, last year,
it was great. Me and Daz Horne decided to run away,
to seek our fortune. We was going to go to London. It
was a Tuesday, I think. But it could have been a
Thursday. No, no, it was a Tuesday, 'cos we had Mr
Cooper for technical drawing. Mr Cooper's soft, sir,
you can swear at him and all sorts, we used to call
him 'gibbon head', 'cos he had a bald head and
looked like a gibbon. Anyway, me and Daz are in his
class and I throws a chair at him, so he goes and hides
himself in a storeroom, so me and Horney lock him in
the storeroom, and then we get a chair and stand on it
and look at him through the window in the top of the
storeroom, and I keeps shouting 'gibbon head' to him
. . . Anyway, then we twags it and gets a bus to the
station. I couldn't stop laughing, sir, honest, just the
picture of gibbon head in that storeroom killed me off.
Anyway, Horney says that we've got drama with Mrs
Hugill before dinner, so we comes back to do our
drama lesson. In drama we did 'different visions of
hell'. I was a cyclops and Horney was my mam.
Anyway, me and Horney got into stacks of trouble. But
I liked doing plays when Mrs Hugill was here . . . Sir,
as far as I know sir, Mr Cooper is still locked in the
storeroom . . .

Gail   He's a liar . . .

Nixon   That was good, Peter. The kids had raw

potential, but I had to get them into plays. They were a funny bunch, but I think they liked me, and I liked them. Whitewall wasn't so bad.

Gail Sir? Can we do *ET*?

Hobby ⎫
Gail ⎭ (*together*) ET, phone home . . .

Music.

The staff-room.

Nixon After the first month I was beginning to feel fairly confident. And I also had my eye on Jackie Prime, PE mistress.

Prime Jackie Prime was tall, sun-tanned, bouncy and an expert at netball and tennis . . . She was developing dance in the gym and took an interest in all games.

Nixon Morning.

Prime Morning.

Nixon How did the first-eleven get on?

Prime Lost sixty-seven nil. Saint George's team are in a different class . . . and Oggy Moxon, our captain, was sent off for spitting.

Nixon Who's Oggy Moxon?

Prime He's the best player we've got. But he's a handful.

Nixon I see.

Prime Have you tasted the coffee? It's like something brought back from a field trip.

Nixon It was eight pence and was forced down you by Madge the tea-lady.

Prime We have our own kettle in the gym. For PE staff only.

Parry   Morning.

Teacher A
Teacher B } *(together)*   Morning, Mrs Parry.

Parry   Morning, Mr Nixon. I hope you're still thinking about *The Mikado*. I wouldn't want your mind to wander on to other things.

Nixon   Don't worry, Mrs Parry, I'll be at rehearsals.

Parry   Good, Mr Nixon. Good. Did you know Whitewall has a farm?

Prime   Well it's not actually a farm Mrs Parry, we do have a pig.

Parry   My dear Miss Prime, we have a number of pigs.

Prime   One's an old sow.

Nixon   And geese?

Parry   Two geese.

Nixon   I was doing duty around the back of the canteen, I was attacked by the geese ... But I have discovered how to avoid the smokers, simply look the other way ...

Prime   Look I must go, I've got baths. It's fairly obvious where the kids are going to smoke, and if you want to catch the smokers you can, but if I was you, I wouldn't go behind the sports hall ...

Nixon   Why?

Prime   That's Oggy Moxon's patch. All the staff leave Oggy well alone.

Nixon   And then she left. She was a breath of fresh air ... A bubble in an otherwise flat brew ... Oh God ... I was becoming infatuated with Jackie Prime.

Gail   But Jackie Prime didn't see Nixon as anything at all. When she looked, he wasn't there, he was just another teacher and she was being sociable.

Jones   You can't sit there, that's Marcus' seat.

Nixon   What about over here?

Jones   That's someone's seat. Frank Collier's.

Nixon   Oh, right. Is this anyone's paper?

Whitham   Yes. It's Deany's, he's on the loo . . .

Nixon   I can't share a cheek on the edge of that, can I, Mavis?

Jones   Sorry, Jeff . . .

Nixon   Even after seven weeks finding a regular seat in the staff-room was a nightmare. I was told by Mr Dean that a lot of new staff preferred to stand outside in the rain. Mr Sawyer had been at Whitewall's for two years and not ever got a seat in the staff-room.

Whitham   I do not believe he is doing this. Look at the timetable, Basford's gone bananas.

Nixon   I longed to be down in the gym and have a cup of tea with Jackie Prime. But – it was a forlorn fantasy.

Whitham   The man does not care, he just doesn't care.

Jones   What's the matter, Maureen?

Whitham   I'm on cover for Mick Edward's remedial English group. I hate them. I do. I hate that group . . .

Jones   I know what you mean . . . I've just had Trisha Foreshore, if that girl says 'I'm bored, miss' once again I'll ring her soddin' neck.

Whitham   But they hate me, he knows they do. It's not fair . . .

Jones Do you know what she says . . . We're looking at the digestive system, and she says 'Miss, the oesophagus is one long tube running from mouth to anus.' I said 'Very good, Trisha, how did you find that out?' She says 'Miss, I went to the dentist and he looked in my mouth and he could tell that I'd got diarrhoea.' I said 'It's pyorrhoea, girl, pyorrhoea, bleeding gums . . .' I give up on some of 'em, I really do . . .

Whitham Remedial English. He knows I've got a doctorate and he puts me on remedial English.

Nixon There was another big fight at break-time. Silly sods.

Music.

Back of the sports hall.

Gail The cock of Whitewall High was Bobby Moxon, known to all and sundry as –

Salty – Oggy Moxon.

Gail There was no doubt at all that Oggy was dangerous, all the teachers gave him a wide berth. He was sixteen going on twenty-five, rumour had it that he had lost his virginity when he was ten and that Miss Prime fancied the pants off him.

Hobby When Oggy Moxon said 'shit', you did, when he said it was Wednesday, it was Wednesday.

Gail One Wednesday, I was stood outside one of the mobile classrooms, Mr Dean had sent me out of the class. I'd told him that I thought Peter the Great was a bossy gett!! And he sent me out . . . I'm stood there with a mood on when Oggy comes past.

Salty *becomes* **Oggy Moxon**.

Oggy All right, Gail?

Gail Yeh. I knew that he fancied me.

Oggy What you doing?

Gail Waiting for Christmas, what's it look like?

Oggy I'm having a party in my dad's pub, wanna come? Most of the third year is coming . . . Should be a good night . . .

Gail Might come then.

Oggy Might see you there.

Gail Might.

Oggy Wear something that's easy to get off. Your luck might be in.

Gail I hate him.

Hobby I do.

Gail Somebody ought to drop him.

Hobby Who? All the staff shit themselves when they have to teach him.

Gail Oggy Moxon's speech about being hard: I'm Oggy Moxon . . . We said you'd have to use your imaginations . . . I'm Oggy, I'm as hard as nails, as toe-capped boots I'm hard, as marble in a church, as concrete on your head I'm hard. As calculus I'm hard. As learning Hebrew is hard, then so am I. Even Basford knows I'm rock, his cane wilts like an old sock . . . And if any teachers in the shitpot school with their degrees and bad breath lay a finger on me, God be my judge, I'll have their hides . . . And if not me, our Nobby will be up to this knowledge college in a flash . . . All the female flesh fancy me in my 501s, no uniform for me never. From big Mrs Grimes to pert Miss Prime I see their eyes flick to my button-holed flies. And they know like I that no male on this staff could satisfy them like me, 'cos I'm hard all the time.

Last Christmas dance me and Miss Prime pranced to
some bullshit track and my hand slipped down her
back, and she told me she thought that I was great, I
felt that arse, that schoolboy wank, a tight-buttocked,
Reebok-footed, leggy-arse . . . I touched that and heard
her sigh . . . for me. And as I walk my last two terms
through these corridors of sickly books and boredom
. . . I see grown men flinch and fear . . . In cookery
one day my hands were all covered with sticky paste,
and in haste I asked pretty Miss Bell if she could get
for me a hanky from my pockets, of course she would,
a student on teaching practice – wanting to help, not
knowing my pockets had holes and my underpants
were in the wash . . . 'Oh no,' she yelped, but in truth
got herself a thrill, and has talked of nothing else these
last two years . . . Be warned, when Oggy Moxon is
around get out your cigs . . . And lock up your
daughters . . .

Music plays. **Gail** *and* **Hobby** *pick up a chair each; they are
about to put the chairs on the desks at the end of a lesson.*
Nixon *puts on his coat. They buttonhole him, they want to talk
to him. He hangs around, really wanting to be elsewhere.*

Gail   Sir, are teachers rich?

Nixon (*as if in anguish*)   Noooo!

Gail   What about Mrs Parry, she's got a massive car?

Nixon   She might be, but I'm not.

Hobby   Are you married, sir?

Nixon (*another difficult response*)   No. Next question.

Hobby *and* **Gail** *try and think of another question which will
have the effect of keeping* **Nixon** *talking to them. Meanwhile he
picks up his briefcase.*

Gail   Sir, is this a school for thickies?

Nixon   Why?

Gail   'Cos when we're going home, all the kids from the posh school, Saint George's . . . ask us if we can add up, and they ask us if we've got any table-tennis homework?

Hobby   Sir, all the kids who go to that school are snobs . . . Their dads drive big cars . . .

Gail   And they call us 'divvies' . . .

Hobby   Sir, because they go there they think they're better than us.

Gail   And, they say our teachers are shit. Oh sorry, didn't mean to say that.

Hobby   Mr Basford's sons go there, don't they?

Gail   Yeh, two twins. 'Twinnies' they're called. They're right brainy . . . Sir, have you got a girlfriend?

Nixon   Not at the moment.

Gail   Brilliant.

Hobby   Do you like it at this school, sir?

Nixon   Yeh, it's OK, you lot are awkward, but OK.

Hobby   Sir, what do you think it's most important for a teacher to do?

Nixon   Well, I think a teacher should have a good relationship, if he hasn't got a relationship he can only ever be a teacher, never a person.

Gail   What about Mr Basford, he hasn't got a good relationship with the kids . . .

Nixon   Well I can't speak for Mr Basford, can I?

Hobby   Sir, the bell's gone . . .

Nixon   You'd better go and get it then – and go quietly. (*A pause.*) It was a trip to see *The Rocky Horror Show* that got me really close to those three, although I had to watch my step with Gail, she kept putting her hand on my leg during the sexy bits . . .

Hobby   Science fiction . . . Whooooo. Double feature.

Gail   Doctor X has built a creature.

Hobby *becomes* **Mr Basford**.

Nixon   Mr Basford you wanted to see me?

Basford   Mr Nixon, I understand you took a group of fifteen-year-olds to see a play featuring transvestites from Transylvania? I can imagine what educational value that has.

Nixon   A black mark from Basford. Mrs Parry had omitted to tell me about the joys of doing cover . . . Usually a student would appear like the ghost of Caesar and present you with a pink slip. This would tell you where to go and who to cover for. Mr Basford was in charge of the cover rota.

Basford   Nixon NI to cover for Fisher FI third-year games . . . And the best of luck.

The gymnasium.

Prime   All right, all third-year deadlegs from Mr Fisher's group shut up, said Miss Jackie Prime. If you want to watch the nineteen seventy-four World Cup Final on video go to the lecture theatre with Mr Clarke's group. Those who want to play pirates in the gym get changed, you without kit better see Mr Nixon.

Hobby   A whole line of kids wearing anoraks came forward . . . Mr Nixon looked staggered, he'd been left to deal with PE's cast-offs.

Gail   And amongst the throng was the legendary Barry Wobschall. Barry never did sport. He hated games.

Hobby   Barry was fifteen but had the manner of an old man. He lived with his grandad and spoke with all the wisdom of someone four times his age. Every day for the past two years he had worked on a milk round.

Nixon   Where's your kit?

Ron   Sir, my shorts don't fit me.

Nixon   What about you?

Piggy   Sir, my mother put my shorts in the wash and they got chewed up because the washer has gone all wrong . . .

Nixon   Oh yeh.

Piggy   It's true, sir, honest.

Nixon   What about you, Barry Wobschall, have you got any kit?

Barry   No, sir.

Piggy   He never brings any kit, sir.

Nixon   I wasn't asking you, was I, Simon Patterson.

Piggy   No, sir.

Nixon   What about a note, Barry? Have you brought a note?

Barry   Sir.

Nixon   Oh let's have it then.

Gail   Barry handed him the note. It was small and crumpled. Barry looked in innocence as Nixon opened the piece of paper.

Gail *hands* **Nixon** *a piece of paper.*

Nixon (*reading*)   'Please leave four pints and a yoghurt this Saturday.'

Barry   It's the only note I could get, sir.

Nixon   I tried to talk Barry Wobschall into changing his options. His sort of humour in a drama class would have been dynamite. But he wouldn't change, he said he preferred doing geog, because it was peaceful and he liked copying maps.

Gail   On the thirteenth of October Jackie Prime was at the GCSE meeting held at Saint George's ... She was walking around the quadrant. A choir was singing.

A choir sings.

Nixon   It's beautiful.

Prime   There's been ...

Nixon   It's just a different world. I hear they're opting out.

Prime   It's very likely. They've got a fantastic drama studio, dance facilities.

Nixon   If they opt out they'll charge fees ... It'll be like a private school.

Prime   They say that they won't, but maybe they will. Only time will tell.

Nixon   Mr Basford's kids come here.

Prime   You sound surprised ... And Jackie Prime was off, into Saint George's gymnasium.

Nixon   It was fantastic. There was something reassuring about Saint George's that made you want to teach there. Something soothing and academic, the same, I was beginning to think, could not be said of Whitewall.

The choir stops.

Back of the sports hall. **Gail**, *as* **Dennis**, *and* **Hobby**, *as* **Oggy Moxon**, *are flicking through a magazine.*

Dennis   Where did you get it?

Oggy   My dad gets 'em delivered in brown paper parcels ...

Dennis   'S have a look.

Oggy   It's disgusting . . .

Dennis   What is, what is?

Hobby   Oggy had stolen one of his father's dirty magazines, for fifty pence third-years could have a quick look. For a quid first-years could have a glance.

Gail   It was break and Oggy and Dennis are sharing a few cigs and a finger through Oggy's dad's magazine.

Nixon   What're you doing, lads?

Oggy   Nothing . . . I'm Oggy.

Nixon   Well, you're obviously doing something.

Oggy   No we're not.

Nixon   You're not smoking, are you?

Dennis   No.

Oggy   What if we are?

Nixon   It'll stunt your growth, you know?

Oggy   So what?

Nixon   What have you got there?

Oggy   A book.

Nixon   I know it's a book.

Oggy   It's my dad's so if I was you I'd leave it with us.

Nixon   Well I think that I'm going to have to report you.

Oggy   Good. You do that.

Nixon   You know what that means, don't you?

Oggy   Yeh, I'll get kicked out of school with any

luck. Great. I don't want to be here, anyway.

Gail   By this time a massive crowd had gathered. Various voices shouted, 'Smack him, Oggy. He's only a drama teacher.'

Nixon   I think you'd better come with me to see Mr Basford.

Oggy   Big deal, he's not going to do anything.

Nixon   Oh, really?

Oggy   Yeh, really.

Nixon   Well we'll see about that. I might have to deal with you myself.

Oggy   What you gonna do, sir? Pretend I'm a tree?

Nixon   I'm going to have to report you.

Oggy   That's tough of you, why don't you have a go with me now, just me and you?

Nixon   I'm going to have to report you.

Oggy   You do that, sir . . .

Nixon   And I turned and walked away, with kids jeering and shouting in the background. And very faintly I heard Oggy Moxon say . . .

Oggy   You wanker . . .

Nixon   It was my first horrific confrontation. I'd played it all wrong . . . I couldn't deal with Oggy. And if I couldn't, who I thought was fairly streetwise, what about Mrs Grimes, or Julie Sharpe or those nice quiet supply teachers who never have a wrong word for anyone?

Hobby   As Nixon walked back to report Oggy, he started to think about getting out of teaching. He started to wish his probationary year away . . .

Nixon   I wasn't talking to you. I was talking to Paul Drewitt, now will everyone hush down? I shan't say it again. All right, we'll wait till everyone's quiet before we go home.

Piggy   Sir, the bell's gone.

Nixon   I know the bell's gone, Simon Patterson, and I'm not bothered, I can stay here all night!

Gail *exits. Music.*

The drama club.

Nixon   During September I held 'drama club' in the school hall after four o'clock. Salty, Gail and Hobby were regulars, we did all sorts of work. But it didn't really meet with the approval of Doug, the caretaker.

Nixon *and* **Hobby** *play some scenes from 'The Witches' in* Macbeth. **Gail**, *as* **Doug** *the caretaker, enters.*

Doug   Come on let's have you, Niko, time to go home. I thought you lot were withdrawing good will? Come on it's half-five let's have you. Time to go find a space somewhere else.

Nixon   Just five more minutes, Doug?

Doug   No come on . . . I've got this floor to buffer. Mrs Parry's got a *Mikado* rehearsal tonight for principals. And I've got the mobiles to do for night class, and then the sports hall, 'cos five-a-side's on tonight. And somebody's gone crackers in the sixth-form bogs . . .

Nixon   Just give us a few more minutes, Doug . . .

Doug   A few more minutes? Bloody hell, where would I be if I gave all the staff a few more minutes?

Nixon   Come on, Doug, don't be such an ogre.

Doug   I'm asking you to leave, that's all.

Nixon But it's the manner of it . . .

Doug I've got to get this buffered that's all I'm bothered about . . .

Nixon It's taken me ages to get these interested in doing a play – do us a favour, give me another twenty minutes . . .

Doug I can't, Mr Nixon . . . We're short-staffed . . . I've got three cleaners off and Jim's back's playing him up . . . I'm only doing my job.

Nixon I'm only trying to do mine.

Doug Look, you don't get paid for this, get yourself off home . . .

Nixon I bet you wouldn't get Basford out of his office . . .

Doug You should have a proper room for this drama thing. I mean doing it in the hall it's a digrace . . . Sometimes I can't get a shine on the floor, I have to polish it . . . And that's a bloody job.

Nixon If you can tell me, Doug, where there is any morsel of space for me to do drama I'd be happy to move. Is there . . . Eh?

Doug Well, it's not worth bloody doing.

Nixon There isn't anywhere . . . I've got the main hall and that's it.

Doug If you ask me they should take it off the bloody timetable, I mean, they don't do any writing make as much noise as they bloody like, waste of Education Authority's bloody money if you ask me.

Nixon You, silly old sod, you don't know what you're talking about.

Doug That's swearing, nobody swears at me, I don't get paid to be bloody sworn at. Wait till I tell Mr Basford.

Doug *moves upstage. Music.*

The staff-room.

Nixon Thursday, November the ninth. Staff-room. One of my biggest fears was that I was teaching the wrong book at O level. I had been doing *Twelfth Night* for ten weeks when I heard a rumour on the grapevine that the actual set book was *The Winter's Tale*. Mr Basford put me right on that, he also put me right on some other things.

Hobby *becomes* **Mr Basford**.

Basford I hear that you've had a bit of a run-in with Doug. Don't upset the caretakers, Jeff, they do a great job.

Nixon I suppose we're all trapped in the same system. Kids. Staff. Caretakers. How are your lads doing at Saint George's?

Basford Fine.

Nixon You live out that way?

Basford Me? No. I live down Greenacre Parade.

Nixon That's this school's catchment area.

Basford That's right . . .

Nixon Why didn't they come to this school?

Basford (*after a pause*) Saint George's get people into Oxford. Thirty per cent get five or more O levels that's why. Fifteen per cent get four here at Whitewall. Parents have the right to choose schools, and I'm choosing.

Nixon But Saint George's is ten miles away . . . It must cost a fortune . . .

Basford I'm making sure my kids have the best

possible education.

Nixon   And you can afford it. What about kids like
Gail Saunders, can their parents pay for them to travel
to Saint George's? No. They can't even afford to pay
out for a school trip . . .

Basford   So what am I supposed to do, make my
lads disadvantaged because others are? Waken up, Jeff.
Parents have a right to send kids to the school of their
choice.

Nixon   And kids have a right to a good education
regardless of whether their parents have the ability or
willingness to choose for them . . . You know as well as
I do that a lot of parents don't attach a great deal of
importance to education, that doesn't mean that we
ditch their kids . . .

Basford   Listen Mr Nixon . . . When you have any
family, what will you want for your kids? Will you
want them to do drama, let's say, in an old hall with
no facilities and books that are sellotaped together or
would you prefer they worked in an atmosphere where
everything was new, and you could have what you
wanted? You think about what you'd really want.

Nixon   But that's not the point. Surely all schools
should be the same, have the same facilities, have the
same cash, cash made readily available. Shouldn't we
want the best for all kids, not just those whose parents
can pay to send them to a good school whether it be
fees or bus fare? All kids deserve the right to be
educated to their potential.

Basford   And that's the sort of system we have now.
A grade-six kid is grade six potential.

Nixon   That's bullshit and you know it. Examinations
are a framework that we fit kids into.

Basford   Do not talk to me like that, Mr Nixon.

Nixon   And don't talk to me like that, you bloody fascist . . .

Basford   I knew what you were as soon as I saw you.

Nixon   What are you talking about?

Basford   You know what I'm talking about, I'm talking about *The Mikado*.

Nixon   What about it . . . ?

Basford   Eight years I've been in that society.

Nixon   And then he stormed off . . .

Whitham   'You've had it now,' said Maureen Whitham, scale-two humanities, as she sat listening and thumbing through *The Times Ed*. Old Basford will make your life a misery, he'll have you on cover from now till eternity. Nobody calls Basford a fascist and gets away with it. The man's dangerous, I'd be careful tackling him. He's done a lot for the school. And after all they're his kids, he can do what he likes . . .

Nixon   I felt that I was wrong, that we shouldn't have a fair system, that we should let bright kids get bright and treat the less able kids like rhubarb, keep them in the dark and shit on 'em. And everywhere I looked I could see the difference between dog piss in Hobby's grandma's garden and garden parties and degrees at Saint George's. And the truth was that the garden party was what I wanted . . . Whitewall was killing me, sapping me, frustrating me – wearing me down . . . As Christmas approached I fell into a deep depression, I had two hundred first-year reports to do, O level marking and the Christmas carol concerts meant that I couldn't get in the hall to teach.

Whitham   Hey, Jeff, have you seen *The Times Ed*? Scale two going at Saint George's. Starts summer. A level theatre studies, drama studio . . . Video equipment . . .

Nixon   No I'm not into that.

Whitham   Oh you're not planning to stop here, are you? Everybody's trying to get out. They call this place Colditz at the County Hall. Don't be a mug, Jeff, when you see a hole in the fence go for it. I've got an interview coming up, in local radio . . . Here, I'll leave it with you.

Hobby   Mr Nixon?

Gail   Sir?

Hobby   Can I go to matron?

Nixon   Look, come away from the gas taps.

Hobby   Sir?

Nixon   Just find a space.

Gail   Sir, she's hit me.

Hobby   Sir, I haven't.

Nixon   Find a space.

Gail   Sir, she has.

Hobby   When will we be back in the hall?

Nixon   Find a space!

Gail   Are we doing the *Marat-Sade*?

Hobby   Can I go to matron?

Gail   Are we doing *Billy Liar*?

Hobby   Sir, she's taken my pen.

Gail   Sir, I haven't.

Hobby   Sir, she has, sir.

Gail   Sir, I haven't.

Hobby   Sir, she's taken my book.

Gail   Sir, I haven't.

Hobby   Sir, she's taken my partner.

Gail   Sir, I haven't.

Hobby   Sir, she's taken my glasses.

Gail   Sir?

Hobby   Mr Nixon.

Gail   Sir?

Hobby   Niko?

Gail   Jeff?

Hobby   Hey.

Gail   You.

Hobby   Sir.

Nixon (*shouting*)   Right! Everybody, hands on heads, and fingers on lips.

Music. Blackout.

Act Two

Christmas time at Whitewall's. The broom is stuck upside down in a desk upstage. Trimmings, a star and a piece of crêpe paper adorn the broom, which is now a Christmas tree. **Salty**, **Gail** *and* **Hobby** *take time putting up the tree.*

Gail Christmas at Whitewall and love was in the air. All over the school there were Christmas trees and cards and trimmings, and every break-time we would queue up to snog Martin Roebuck under some mistletoe in the reference section of the library.

Hobby Christmas also saw the culmination of Gail's interest in Mr Nixon.

Gail I love him . . .

Hobby You don't.

Gail I do . . . I am infatuated . . .

Hobby What's it feel like?

Gail Brilliant . . . I was on his table for Christmas dinner . . .

Hobby Yeh but does he love you?

Gail Dunno but I'll find out at the Christmas dance . . .

Hobby Why, what are you going to do?

Gail Snog him.

Hobby OOOOOOHHHH, you're not . . .

Gail I'll need some Dutch courage but I am . . .

Hobby I don't believe it . . .

Gail Listen, I've got it all worked out. We go to the off-licence, you go in and buy some cider.

Hobby Why me?

Gail Then I'll bring some spring onions from home. We'll drink the cider then eat the spring onions.

Hobby Spring onions, why?

Gail Because Doug and Mr Hatton will be on the door of the Christmas dance and Mrs Parry says if anyone is suspected of drinking alcohol they won't be allowed in . . . And I want to make sure I get in.

Hobby Are you sure Mr Nixon is going to the dance?

Gail Course he is, I've asked him a dozen times. I've sent him forty cards in the Christmas post.

Hobby Must have cost you a fortune.

Gail No my aunty works in a card shop, anyway it's the thought that counts.

Hobby So I went into the off-licence, and bought two large bottles of cider.

Gail Which we drank through a straw . . . And then we stuffed ourselves with spring onions.

Mr Hatton Bloody hell. Have you been eating spring onions?

Hobby That was Mr Hatton's reaction as we came into the disco . . .

Gail Brilliant we're in, I told you it'd work, I'm slightly merry but not out of control.

Hobby I feel sick. I hate onions.

Gail Salty?

Salty What?

Gail Have you seen Mr Nixon?

Salty No, is he coming? Brilliant.

Gail Is he here yet?

Salty Hey can you smell onions?

Hobby Niko hadn't arrived, he was up in the pub with the rest of the staff, and he was sat very near to Miss Jackie Prime. Meanwhile down at the disco Mr Dean was doing Jimmy Saville impersonations and playing records that were three years out of date . . .

Deanie Yes indeedy this is the sound of the Human League, 'Don't You Want Me Baby . . .'

Gail Oh shit, look out, Oggy Moxon.

Salty *becomes* **Oggy**.

Oggy Got you . . .

Gail Hey oh . . . great . . .

Oggy Giz a kiss then . . .

Gail Haven't you got any mistletoe?

Oggy I don't need mistletoe. Why didn't you come to my party, you owe me one . . .

Gail Later, eh, maybe later . . . I dashed away from Oggy leaving him wondering what perfume smells like onions . . .

Hobby It is a fact of life that all teachers dance like retards. They dance like they're all out of a music documentary . . . It must be the weight of all that knowledge in their heads which makes them look like they're in the back seat of an old Ford Cortina . . . Mr Dean was a supreme example of bad dancing . . .

Deanie Now then, now then what have we here? Uncle Ted, a bit of the old boogie woogie. (*He demonstrates extreme bad dancing.*)

Hobby Oggy?

Salty *becomes* **Oggy** *and kicks someone in the face.* **Hobby** *reacts.*

Hobby   There'd been some trouble in the toilets,
Oggy Moxon had hit Kev Jones for nothing . . .

Gail   Kev said that Oggy hit him because he fancied
me . . . Oggy tried to get me to dance but both times I
left him and went to the toilets . . . (*She moves upstage.*)

Nixon   Simon Patterson, very smart . . . Merry
Christmas.

Hobby   Merry Christmas, sir . . .

Nixon   Where's Salty?

Hobby   I think he's dancing. Gail's in the loo . . .
Have you been drinking, sir?

Nixon   Only a few pints, I'm in my new car.

Hobby   Yeh you need a car when you're drinking
and driving.

Nixon   The Christmas dance had all the seriousness
of a big disco, and the fifteen- and sixteen-year-olds
looked stunning done up to the nines, and only Mr
Moorcroft, Head of RE seemed not to be moved by
the gyrating bottoms and boobs . . . At ten-thirty when
things seemed like they were bubbling Deanie played
the last record, a smoocher and Gail Saunders
appeared in my arms and suddenly my face was
confronted by the strong smell of onion . . .

Salty, *as* **Nixon** *and* **Gail** *smooch.* **Hobby**, *as* **Oggy
Moxon**, *hangs around.*

Gail   It was fantastic . . .

Nixon   It felt rather awkward, I didn't know how
tight to hold Gail or where to put my hands . . .

Parry   Mrs Parry looked on, she felt a mixture of
jealousy and condemnation. But it wasn't unknown for
teachers to dance with students especially at Christmas.

After all, as she had said, students were treated like young adults here at Whitewall.

Gail Doug the caretaker cleared the dance floor in a few minutes. And just as I was going to kiss Mr Nixon, he turned his head to wish Doug –

Nixon (*turning his head*) – a merry Christmas, Doug . . .

Hobby Oggy Moxon had seen Gail and Niko dancing but he left the hall in silence . . .

Gail Mr Nixon said that he would give me a lift down home, Salty and Hobby decided to walk it home and maybe get a kebab . . .

Nixon I got into my car, an A reg Escort, and Gail jumped in beside me, and before I knew it, into the back jumped Oggy Moxon . . .

Hobby *becomes* **Oggy Moxon**.

Oggy Oh yeh, what's all this then? Bit of slap and tickle with the drama teacher, Gail. I thought all drama wallas were puffballs?

Nixon Will you get out, Oggy?

Oggy Will you get out, Oggy? No I will not.

Nixon Get out.

Oggy No, let's go a ride eh . . . ? Drop me down home, will you?

Nixon Get out.

Oggy Make me.

Nixon Get out . . .

Oggy Make me . . .

Nixon I shan't say it again . . .

Oggy I shan't say it again. Come on, sir, make me

get out . . .

Nixon This is my car, I'm not in school hours, now get out . . .

Gail Come on, Oggy . . . It's not fair.

Oggy What's not fair? You want me to go so that you can have Mr Nixon all to yourself?

Nixon I'm going to get Mrs Parry . . .

Oggy What the fuck is she going to do about it?

Nixon Will you get bloody out . . .

Oggy You make me . . .

Nixon Arrgh . . .

Gail Oggy!!

Nixon *hits* **Oggy** *in the face. Screaming,* **Oggy** *pulls himself out of the car.*

Oggy You've broke my nose, you bastard . . .

Gail Mr Nixon . . .

Oggy You bastard . . .

Nixon There was blood everywhere . . .

Gail I was screaming, Nixon was shaking.

Nixon A few members of staff came running from the school . . .

Hobby Oggy staggered away from the car. (*As* **Oggy**.) Our Nobby'll get you Nixon . . . Wait till next term our Nobby'll hammer you. (*Pause.*) And he was off into the dark. It was like a film . . . Everyone was shouting and trying to calm things . . . And in the distance you could hear Oggy Moxon shouting . . . 'I'm gonna do you, Nixon, I'm gonna do you . . .'

Gail As we stood, a boy ran past us and jumped into

his father's car . . . And a voice bellowed out . . .

Nixon   Stop running, Simon Patterson!

Blackout. After a pause the lights come up again.

New Year. The staff-room.

Parry   Morning, Jeff.

Nixon   Morning, Mrs Parry.

Whitham   Happy New Year.

Parry   Happy New Year.

Whitham   Had a nice time?

Nixon   Lovely thanks, we went away . . . (*He starts to dismantle the Christmas tree.*)

Parry   So did we . . .

Whitham   We stayed at home.

Parry   You'll never guess what?

Whitham   Go on.

Parry   Jackie Prime got married, to Colin Short, head of PE from Saint George's, did it over Christmas.

Whitham   I didn't know . . .

Parry   Neither did I . . .

Nixon   What was that?

Parry   For Prime read Short . . . He's a hunk of a fella all man . . .

Nixon   Oh . . . Happy New Year . . .

Parry   You did what, Mr Nixon? Said Mrs Parry. Her yellow dress clashing with her pink blouse.

Nixon   I . . . erm . . . erm . . . headbutted him in the face.

Parry If he decides to report this to the police or to his parents I'm afraid you're for the high jump.

Gail But Oggy Morton didn't report the incident to either his dad or the police, but he told Nobby, and Nobby said that he would fix Nixon.

Nixon During every lesson I had one eye on the main entrance in case Oggy's brother appeared. And I wondered how many staff had said to how many kids 'Bring your dad up' and then wondered all day if they would.

Hobby Three or four days went by and nothing happened, Oggy's brother didn't appear and many teachers winked at Mr Nixon as much as to say 'nice one'.

Music.

Nixon's *bedsit.*

Nixon Most of my nights were spent indoors marking, going over the same mistakes and the same right answers. I was turning into a monk. I lived close to the school so I couldn't go to the local pub. It was full of the sixth form, and I didn't know whether to be all mates or to tell the landlord that they were under age. So I stayed in and listened to Janis Ian and Dire Straits, and waited to see if I'd get an interview at Saint George's . . .

The main hall.

Gail During January the shine seemed to go off Nixon.

Salty And once we heard that he was applying somewhere else we sort of drifted away for a bit . . . But we had a laugh. One day he asked us in drama to do a play about corporal punishment in schools, so we, Hobby, me and Gail did this thing about school killers.

Hobby   Right, in the staff-room there's a red phone, like a batphone, and it glows really red when someone's on the other line.

Gail   And in each classroom under the desk there's a buzzer, so if a teacher gets into some trouble or has a kid who is getting stroppy she can press the buzzer, and the phone rings.

Salty   Right, in the staff-room, just like sat about all day drinking coffee, and reading ancient books are these ninjas, Japanese martial arts experts, who are trained to kill kids, with karate chops or sharp stars that they throw. And in the staff-room are a number of wires, so that these ninjas –

Hobby   – when they get the call –

Salty   – can jump out of the window of the staff-room and be at the root of the problem in a few seconds . . .

Gail   Right I'm the French assistant, and I'm teaching . . .

Hobby   I'm Rachael Steele – and I throw something at the board.

Gail   (*with a French accent*)   Who was that . . . Who was that who was throwing missiles towards my head? This is very dangerous and could be if someone gets hurt . . . Was it you, Rachael?

Hobby   What, miss?

Gail   You know what.

Hobby   No I don't, you frog . . .

Gail   And then suddenly the French assistant presses the buzzer for insolence.

Salty   The phone rings . . .

Hobby   The ninjas are in action . . . Out of the staff-room window, coffee all over the place . . .

Gail   Five seconds later . . . They arrive, kick the
door down, tear gas all over the place . . .

Hobby   The teacher had a mask secreted in her desk.

Gail   Merci, ninja . . .

Salty   Bonjour.

Gail   The French assistant is back at work . . .

Hobby   A call is made to Mr and Mrs Steele, would
they like to come and collect the remains of their
daughter Rachael from the school morgue. She was
killed during a French lesson. Thank you . . .

Nixon   It was stories like that, which kept me, Jeff
Nixon, alive at Whitewall. And to my surprise the kids
in drama got better and better, their imagination knew
no bounds . . .

Gail   You can't teach imagination, can you, sir?

Nixon   I don't know . . .

Gail   When was the battle of Hastings?

Nixon   Ten sixty-six.

Gail   What can you do with a brick?

Nixon   Eh?

Gail   What can you do with a brick? I saw this in a
magazine . . .

Nixon   Build a house . . .

Gail   Yeh and . . . ?

Nixon   Throw it.

Gail   That shows the violent side of you. You can do
unlimited things with a brick. You can drill a hole in it
and wear it around your neck . . . You could marry a
brick . . .

Hobby   My cousin married a prick.

Gail   There's lots of different answers. It says in this magazine that you can exercise your imagination, that's what we do in drama.

Hobby   And art . . .

Gail   Yeh but we don't do it in much else, do we? We're like robots. Who invaded England in ten sixty-six? Arm up, Norman the Conqueror. Arm down, computer programme complete.

Music.

Mrs Parry's *office.*

Nixon   On January the twenty-first Mrs Parry called me to her office. She said it was urgent. Oggy has pressed charges, I knew it.

Parry   Jeff. Thank God you're here.

Nixon   What's the matter, is it Oggy Moxon?

Parry   Worse.

Nixon   His brother . . . Nobby . . . He's come to fix me?

Parry   No. Can you do Koko? Mr Gill, who had the part slipped a disc last night building the set. Can you step into the breach, Jeff? I'd regard it as a great personal favour?

Nixon   What about asking Mr Basford?

Parry   Derek Basford is never a Koko, Jeff.

Nixon   But I'm in the chorus.

Parry   You can do that as well, do it for me, Jeff . . . You can't let me down, Jeff Nixon.

Nixon   And so it was that Mrs Parry got me to play Koko.

Parry   Wonderful, wonderful, we rehearse Wednesdays and Sunday . . . See you Sunday.

Gail   When Mr Basford heard the news he went barmy with the cover rota.

Nixon   And for the next three weeks, I was on cover all the time, French, German, physics, childcare, rural studies, needlework.

Music.

The Mikado *rehearsals.*

Parry   Pick your teeth up, Mr Dean . . . Just pick them up and carry on singing . . . Move left, dear, move left . . . Good . . . There's no need to slouch in the chorus, Mr Basford. Remember you are gentlemen of Japan not lepers. Dignity.

Nixon   Three members of the chorus were smoking.

Parry   Carry on, carry on . . .

Nixon   Mrs Parry's last production, *The Pirates*, lasted eight and a half hours . . . This looks like it could be longer . . .

Doug   Face the front . . . Sing out front . . .

Parry   Stay on stage, don't come out and watch, stay in the wings . . . It's no good saying 'I was just coming to watch this bit', stay on stage . . .

Nixon   The stage was a cattle market . . .

Parry   Carry on, carry on, just do it . . .

Nixon   But for Mrs Parry it was close enough for jazz.

Parry   Amateurs, Mr Nixon, never work with animals, children and amateurs.

Nixon I'm sure it'll be ... erm ... great, Mrs Parry.

Parry I do hope so, Mr Nixon. This is my fifth *Mikado*, I haven't quite got it right yet ... But we're trying. Do you know your lines yet?

Nixon Yes.

Parry Oh ... Well, marvellous.

Nixon Would you like me to get up and do my bit?

Parry Oh no, if you know your lines you needn't bother coming till the dress rehearsal, I know you'll be brilliant ... OK everyone, let's press on, where's the Mikado, where's Poo-bah, where's Nanky Poo?

Doug They're in the music room playing bridge.

Parry Well tell them that I need them NOW!

Doug Oi ... you're bloody on ...

Nixon During February the mock exams were held in the main hall.

Doug Doug, the caretaker was as smug as a Cheshire cat. Haha you'll not be able to do any drama now, Niko ... Basford's scotched you this time. Seven weeks these desks have got to stay in here ... He could have put these in the gym but Dave Fisher asked him not to ...

Nixon It's OK, Doug, I'm going to do all my drama classes in the back room of the George and Dragon.

Doug I hope you get that job at Saint George's ... Let them have a basinful of you ...

Nixon I reckon that I could teach drama anywhere and no one would mind. In the cookery class.

The class scream. They are improvising around the Marat-Sade. **Gail** *tells the audience she is Jean-Paul Marat.*

Hobby In the coal bunker ...

Salty   In the boiler house . . .

Gail   Canteen . . .

Hobby   Sports hall showers . . .

Salty   School gates . . .

Gail   Swimming baths . . .

Hobby   Woolworth's . . .

Salty   Simon Patterson's bedroom.

All   Stop running, Simon Patterson.

Nixon   What I couldn't fathom is why a school didn't have a space that was solely used for exams. You would have thought that somewhere along the way from the first paper ever sat at Oxford that some boffin would have seen that schools need purpose-built rooms to do exams in. But then what did I know?

Parry   You knew that you'd got an interview at Saint George's . . . Congratulations, said Mrs Parry.

Nixon   She was one of my referees. So joining the G and S had its advantages. But rumour had it that Basford wrote all references and I knew he'd be happy to see me go. Drama didn't feature in his scheme of things.

Hobby *becomes* **Mr Basford**.

Basford   Mr Nixon, can I ask you to keep the noise down? I've got a sixth-form group in the lecture theatre, we can't hear ourselves think.

Nixon   You what, Mr Basford?

Basford   It's like an asylum in here.

Nixon   Yeh great, isn't it? They've really taken to it. We're doing the *Marat-Sade*. It's set in a bath house.

Basford   Quiet. Keep them quiet. I said keep the

noise down.

Nixon   Hang on, Mr Basford, I wouldn't do that to you.

Basford   It's like a flaming riot.

Nixon   They're enjoying themselves.

Basford   Enjoying themselves? They sound like they're screaming to get out of your lesson, they can't stand it.

Nixon   I'm sure that there's more sixth formers screaming to get out of yours . . .

Basford   Watch your step, Nixon.

Nixon   He was pissed off because I'd got an interview. Apparently, according to Mr Dean, he had applied for the head at Saint George's job and had not had his references taken up . . . It had made him a bitter man . . .

Music.

Saint George's private school.

Ms Coates   Well thank you very much, Mr Nixon, it's been a pleasure talking to you. Obviously we have other candidates to see but we should be able to let you know either way before the end of spring term.

Mrs Clifton   His interview at Saint George's had gone very well. Mrs Clifton, one of the governors of Saint George's, thought he would be outstanding. She also thought he would be a marvellous asset to Saint George's Amateur Players, a society run by Mrs Clifton.

Nixon   Saint George's was a sanctuary compared with Whitewall, kids stood up when a teacher went into class, no one leaped for the door when the bell rang, and their drama studio was pure heaven, I was told

that the caretaker at Saint George's often sat in and
watched drama classes, and not a single person had
walked through the drama studio ever.

Hobby   Chalk and cheese.

Nixon   That's the difference. Unbelievable.

Gail   Colditz Jeff. The great escape.

A choir sings.

Tennis courts.

Gail   One Wednesday when not a lot was happening
Mr Basford had organised a tennis competition. Some
of the third year were allowed out on to the courts.

Salty   You mean *court*.

Gail   Whitewall only had one decent court. The rest
were like dirt tracks.

Salty   Mr Nixon had been invited to take part at the
last minute because Mick Edwards had a meeting with
the Social Services.

Hobby   Forty love, game Basford. Hard luck, Mr
Dean.

Gail   Mr Dean got thrashed and so he took his class
back to the mobiles to study the unification of
Germany, he was a bad loser.

Hobby   Forty love, game Basford. Bad luck, Mr
Fisher, you've got bowlegs. Couldn't stop a pig in a
ginnel . . .

Gail   Mr Basford was an ace tennis player, Jackie
Prime told me that he was a county player in his
youth.

Salty   He had no kit, he looked like Barry Wobschall.
Borrowed a pair of pumps from big Pete Saxon and
Salty lent him some shorts . . . Somehow, mysteriously,

got a bye into the final. And in the final played Mr
Basford, who had annihilated Jackie Prime's husband.
He was glad about that.

Hobby   Bad luck, Mr Short.

Salty   Hey Shorty, too much bed, not enough sleep.
When Nixon came on to the court all the kids were
laughing.

They laugh.

Gail   Niko looked like somebody from Doctor
Barnardo's. Nothing fitted him.

Hobby   Are you sure you know what you're doing,
Mr Nixon?

Nixon   All the kids had their faces pushed against the
wire of the courts.

They pull a face, to show this.

Gail   Go on, Mr Basford, smash the ball through his
head. That was Oggy Moxon.

Hobby   Forty love.

Gail   Smash him, Basford.

Hobby   Game Basford.

Gail   Jackie Prime was smirking the sort of smirk that
only PE staff can do.

Hobby   Game Basford ...

They play tennis by tapping a chair and watching a ball.

Gail   Come on, Mr Basford, humiliate him ...
Shouted Oggy, like a wild animal ...

Salty   And he tried to ... It was like watching
Christians in the Colieseum ...

Hobby   Love all.

Salty   Fifteen love . . .

Hobby   Well done, Mr Nixon. You've won a point. I didn't know you could play.

Nixon   Yeh, what he didn't know, what none of the staff knew was that I was an under-nineteen tennis international . . . And I thrashed Basford. One six, six love, six love..

Gail   Mr Basford left the courts in haste. All the kids looked gob-smacked.

Nixon   I could have spared him, but why should I . . .? As I walked from the courts I bumped into Oggy Moxon . . .

Gail *becomes* **Oggy Moxon**.

Oggy   Our Nobby's gonna fix you.

Nixon   Great.

Oggy   Hey . . . I thought you were a fart . . . Didn't know you could play tennis.

Nixon   Neither did Mr Basford. And you tell your Nobby if he comes up here, I'll shove this down his neck.

Oggy   Right . . . I'll tell him . . .

Music.

Hobby   With the end of term only six weeks off Niko had this idea of me, Gail and Salty doing a play about school life for the leavers.

Salty   It was great because Niko had arranged for us to get out of other lessons, 'cos we didn't have exams.

Gail   And most teachers were happy to let us go . . .

Salty   It was brilliant, like we had the freedom of the city . . . It's great . . . I'm missing maths to do drama, brilliant . . .

Gail   Salty was over the moon. He was running around school like a headless chicken. He had written in spray paint on the side of the gym –

Salty   – Mr Basford is a fat Basford.

Hobby   All the staff thought it was fairly amusing. Basford didn't, he put Salty on a long list of Easter leavers who had to see Mrs Parry . . .

Parry   You don't come to school to fool about, Ian, to waste your time. We treat you like young adults and we expect you to behave accordingly. I don't think that writing swear words on a wall is a mature thing to do. Do you?

Salty   No, Mrs Parry.

Parry   Well why did you do it, Ian?

Salty   Fed up, Mrs Parry.

Parry   Fed up with what? What are you fed up with, Ian?

Salty   Loads of things, Mrs Parry. Having to leave school.

Parry   Well we all have to leave school sometime, don't we?

Salty   Yeh but that's it, Mrs Parry, out there, there's nothing, it's just a load of lies. A load of promises that never happen. I'm sixteen, and I might have wasted my time in school and I've got to bugger off. Maybe I'm not ready for that . . . I've woken up too late, Mrs Parry. I don't want to be a piece of rhubarb . . . I want another chance . . . What's the word I am? I'm a late developer, Mrs Parry, I've got some interest, I've found something I'm interested in – with Mr Nixon. Who is it that says we only have one chance, Mrs Parry? Is it God, 'cos if it is it's not the same God my mother talks about . . .

Parry   Everyone has to grow up, Ian. Leaving school is just a part of growing up.

Salty   Yeh but nobody out there cares. If people did care you'd be able to say to me, 'All right, Salty, stop on, start again, have another crack' . . . I can't negotiate, Mrs Parry, you can't negotiate . . . Who is it who traps us both? Politicians . . . them men on the telly with funny haircuts, them men who talk about choice and equality and fairness . . . Why don't any of them live on our estate? Why don't I see any of them down the welfare hall or at the Bingo? . . . They're not bothered about us . . . Do you believe what they say, Mrs Parry? It's all a load of lies. They don't care, and what's worse, you know, is that they're not bothered that they don't care. Then I turned and left her room.

Parry   Ian Salt, come here immediately . . .

Music.

The staff-room.

Whitham   Congratulations. You did it.

Jones   Well done, Jeff.

Whitham   When do you start?

Nixon   September.

Jones   Another success for the escape committee.

Whitham   We'll have a drink after *The Mikado*, said Maureen Whitham, who was playing Sing Sing. I've got my job in local radio, make it a double celebration.

Nixon   I was obviously very pleased. The kids said that I would change, going to a snob school. But it was an unbelievable feeling. And for some reason Jackie Short, née Prime kissed me . . . I felt like a great weight had been lifted from my shoulders, I could breath once more, I was free . . . Thank God I was free . . .

Jones   Hey, I've got another interview, it's my seventeenth this month.

Whitham   Orrrrr . . .

Nixon   The opening night of *The Mikado* was extra-or-dinary.

Blackout. After a pause, the lights come up again.

Parry   Thank you, thank you.

Gail *presents her with a bouquet.*

Parry   Thank you, thank you all. I'd like if I may to thank everyone concerned. I'd like to thank Gerald my husband for being so patient, and also Daphne and Clarence my two wonderful children, and of course Doug the caretaker, without whom this production would not have been possible. And also all the backstage team . . . Come on, fellas, let's have you out here . . .

Nixon   It was the shortest production of *The Mikado* in history, fifty-five minutes. Forty-six pages of the libretto had been skipped over. But it was still a success.

Parry   And I'd like to thank Simon and Peter for numbering the chairs.

Nixon   The thank-yous went on for an hour.

Parry   And Joyce, Hilda and Francis who did the little buns and cakes, and how lovely they were as well.

Nixon   The cast stood there wilting.

Parry   And Martin and Chris for cutting the squares of cinemoid which made all those lovely colours. And to Desmond and Sue who helped park the cars. Thanks to you all.

Gail On the last night of *The Mikado* Mrs Parry
threw a party in the sixth-form common room.
Everyone chatted and drank Pomagne from paper
cups. Basford was there. (*As* **Basford**.) So, I suppose
it's congratulations, Mr Nixon?

Nixon Sorry?

Basford Congratulations. You must feel very pleased
with yourself?

Nixon Not really.

Basford You were a very good Koko, it was quite a
swan-song.

Nixon Thanks very much, Derek.

Basford I'm sure you'll have a great time over at
Saint George's. It's what you want, isn't it? They're
quite into drama over there. The twins are thinking of
drama as an option. This is not a school for drama,
never has been, never will be.

Nixon I'll miss the kids.

Basford Not for long. You just have a thought for
us, still stuck here. Mind you, every cloud has a silver
lining as they say, Mrs Parry has just asked me if I'd
like to play Nathan Detroit in next term's *Guys and
Dolls*.

Nixon And are you?

Basford My dear boy, the part was made for me.

Hobby All the kids were really sad when Nixon left,
and me and Salty and Gail all cried.

Gail We never saw Niko again. Somebody told us
that he was having a good time at Saint George's, and
that all the posh kids loved him. When we left school I
got a job typing, and I did some dance. I was also in
the chorus of *Guys and Dolls*.

Hobby And I'd got this job with my uncle. And Oggy Moxon . . . it was like on a farm, hard work, but good fun.

Salty I didn't know what to do. I couldn't think anything up. I wanted to write songs for Wham and be a millionaire, but Mr Harrison said it was too far-fetched . . . But I'd like to . . .

A school bell rings. End of school. The lights change. **Salty**, **Gail** *and* **Hobby** *are lost. They move around the stage slowly, and pick up their bags. Silence.*

Gail Oh well . . . that's it then.

Hobby The end.

Salty Mr Harrison, can I just say before we go, sir, don't leave, sir. The kids here need teachers like you. Don't go to that snob school, sir.

Gail Sir, if you stay, we'll come back and bug you. We'll let you know how we're getting on. I'll come and cut your hair if you like . . . I'm doing a scheme at the hairdresser's, it's twenty-five quid but my mam says it's better than nothing. Just.

Salty Sir, I'm doing a scheme, painting and decorating, should be a laugh, I'm crap at art. Might end up on an advert . . . Be a star then, sir . . .

Gail Don't leave, sir . . .

Hobby I'm doing french polishing, gonna hate it.

Salty If you stay and do another drama play, we'll be in it . . .

Hobby Best thing I've ever done at school this . . . It's the only thing I'll remember . . .

Salty We could have a laugh, start a group up.

Gail And rehearse at nights . . .

Salty   Hey we could do all sorts ... *Marat-Sade*.

Gail   Comedics.

Hobby   Tragedies.

Gail   Westerns.

Salty   Kung fu ...

Gail   Sir, romances ...

Hobby   Sex plays ...

Salty   Sir ... I've got it ... Why don't you do *The Mikado* ... ?

Gail   *Mikado*. Sir, you said that was shit.

Hobby   Anyway ... See you, sir ... See you, Mrs Hudson ...

Salty   Yeh. Thanks, sir ...

Gail   Yeh.

Hobby   Yeh thanks.

Salty   Yeh.

Gail   Thanks a lot.

Salty   See you ...

Hobby   Tara ...

Gail   Yeh.

They walk away. They freeze. 'Gentlemen of Japan' from The Mikado *plays.*

Blackout.

Happy Jack

Happy Jack was first presented professionally by Hull Truck Theatre Company in 1985 with the following cast:

Jack   Andrew Livingston
Liz   Jane Clifford

Directed by John Godber

Act One

An empty space. There are two chairs on stage. A backcloth with worn wallpaper gives shape to the stage. An old gramophone is standing at the back of the stage. A clothes rack is full of clothes that the actors will use during the play. Kitty Kallen's 'Little Things Mean a Lot' plays as the audience enters. The actors enter very slowly. The house lights are up and bright light fills the stage. The actors speak directly to the audience.

Liz Blow me a kiss from across the room ...

Jack Say I look nice ...

Liz When I'm not. Brush my hair ...

Jack As you pass my chair.

Liz Little things mean a lot.

Jack *Happy Jack.*

Liz The cast ...

Jack With —— as Jack ...

Liz And —— as Elizabeth.

Jack Page one, the introduction.

Liz Jack Munroe was born in 1914, seventy-odd years ago to this very month. He was the only son of Amanda Munroe and lived all of his life in Upton, a small mining village in the West Yorkshire coalfield. Jack was a miner, a father, a brawler, sometime poet, thug, con-man, lover and comedian.

Jack He was a big chap, about 230 pounds, and over six feet tall. Big for a miner. He started work at Frickley Colliery at the age of fifteen ...

Liz Fourteen.

Jack (*looks at her, and continues*) He came straight out of the Board school and straight into the pit. Some would say he was lucky, he worked through both wars. Jack would say . . .

Liz   'That's the way things 'appen.'

Jack   By the time he was seventeen he had twenty men working under him.

Liz   But he always remained a collier, never went to management.

Jack   In his own two-fisted animal way, Jack commanded respect . . .

Liz   If they didn't respect . . .

Jack   He would hit people. In fact when he was in one of his . . .

Liz   'Moods' . . .

Jack   As Elizabeth would call them, he would hit anyone.

Liz   Even his wife.

Jack   Only when they were first married.

Liz   She was born Elizabeth Cooper.

Jack   They were the same age.

Liz   More or less. They had always known each other . . .

Jack   Lived down the same street . . .

Liz   Carr Lane . . .

Jack   Went to the same school . . .

Liz   Northfield Board School . . .

Jack   They would always be together.

Liz   At the age of twenty-two, when she returned from 'service' in Bradford, they were married.

Jack   He never recalled calling her 'Elizabeth'.

Liz   Always 'Liz'.

Jack   Jack worked at the pit for forty-two years. He was to suffer from knee trouble, kidney trouble and finally pneumoconiosis. The strenuous work of a fit young man, the tests of resilience and feats of strength were to batter his body.

Liz   A fact that he didn't realise until later life.

Jack   The Coal Board awarded him a thousand pounds for his dust.

Liz   That's forty-two years' coal dust on his lungs.

Jack   They lived all their married life in Saxon Terrace. One street in a large area of terraced houses, all pointing in the same direction – towards the pit. In later years the two of them struggled to buy their house, when many of the others had been knocked down.

Liz   The house was spotless. 'Cleanliness . . .'

Jack   Liz would say . . .

Liz   '. . . is next to godliness.' She struggled daily to keep the house in sparkling condition. As the years drew on the house was to become less neat, more lived in, untidy, this was to irritate Liz through her later years. She wasn't up to the sort of cleaning of her 'service' days. In 1975 she died, of a stroke, and despite an operation in her fifties her body was riddled with cancer. She died in hospital, with Jack characteristically by her side.

Jack   She often referred to him as . . .

Liz   'Happy Jack'.

Jack   It was her little joke. Sometimes she used it with tenderness, and sometimes to have a dig at him.

Most of the time she regarded him as 'Pa', but if she wanted something special doing it would be 'Jacko'. Her favourite and lasting expression though was 'Happy Jack'. She felt quite pleased at awarding him this title. He was always miserable or, more to the point, appeared to be so.

Liz It was a quirk of the Munroe household that you didn't express any love or caring or affection directly to anyone who you happened to love or care for. Jack was a master at this, and had developed it further.

Jack So much so that the person who you loved the most you demonstrated the most disdain and contempt for.

Liz But beneath it all, over the years, there had been enough love to sink a mine shaft.

Jack Neither would admit that.

Liz In 1978, three years after Liz, Jack died.

Jack Those years almost killed him. He was to diminish in stature as well as spirit.

Liz For the first time he had to make decisions, to make his meals, make the beds, collect the pension and sleep alone.

Jack His health deteriorated.

Liz After having walked fifty yards, he would be out of breath; going upstairs to bed would leave him exhausted; often he would lay awake at nights crying for Elizabeth and trying to catch his breath.

Jack He refused to move into a bungalow, and lived at Saxon Terrace until he had forcibly to be moved to his daughter's, where he died. Of a stroke. His kidneys had collapsed. Years of hard physical graft had taken their toll.

Liz He was a wreck.

Jack   He was dead.

Liz   He was buried next to Elizabeth and they shared the same headstone, just as they had shared everything else.

Jack   If you were to ask Jack, 'Would you do it all again?'

Liz   I'm sure he'd say ...

Jack   Yes.

Liz   Page six, scene one. The Munroes' household. Two large easy chairs and a gramophone. Jack is seated, he is ...

Jack   Sixty-one.

Liz   And Elizabeth.

Jack   Liz.

Liz   Is sixty. They are sat in the dark listening to a collection of their favourite records. They are very content and relaxed. Jack may sing to the records. Liz sits by the fire and gazes into the range, watching the shapes that the flames make. They often sat like this, thinking of the years together.

Jack   Little things mean a lot.

Liz   They would play all their favourites, Steve Conway, Bing, the Ink Spots ...

Jack   Louis Armstrong.

Liz   Louis Armstrong, Dean Martin ...

Jack   Al Jolson ...

Liz   Al Jolson, Alma Cogan, Johnny Ray.

Jack   Jack's favourite singing star of all was ...

Liz   Mario Lanza.

Jack They would sit for hours and listen to Mario sing . . .

The lights have gone dim during the last sequence. The actors are 'in' the Munroes' living room. Mario Lanza singing 'Golden Days' plays. **Jack** *and* **Liz** *may sing to some of it.*

Jack Beautiful. Tha can't lick Mario for singin'. I once thought that John Hanson was good but, I've gi' o'er.

Liz He is good, but he's gerrin' on a bit now is John Hanson.

Jack Who, Mario?

Liz John Hanson.

Jack Wi' Mario it comes easy. Mind you, it went to his head.

Liz And he got fat.

Jack What?

Liz Mario got fat.

Jack He was fat in *The Great Caruso*. Fat as a pig.

Liz That was why he couldn't be the prince.

Jack Eh?

Liz In *The Student Prince*. He was too bloody fat. Would've looked a bit daft having a fat prince. Big fat pig. It was his voice that did the singing though, but he was too fat for a prince. You don't see any fat princes.

Jack Great film.

Liz 'Golden Days', Jacko. Can you remember?

Jack I bloody can.

Liz When he goes back to Kathy at the Inn, where he's been a student, and he can't marry her, coz he's a prince. Well . . . I cried my bloody eyes out.

Jack Good film.

Liz Cried for an hour.

Jack Mind you, tha can't lick Mario.

Liz I've allus liked John Hanson.

Jack He's not a patch on Mario.

Liz Ohhh, but he's good though.

Jack He ought to pack it in, did John Hanson.

Liz Can you remember when we saw him at Leeds Grand? Eee, it wa' a laugh.

Jack He wa' int *Desert Song* then, Liz.

Liz Wa' he? Oh, aye, he wa', Pa, you're right.

Jack He wa' t' Red Shadow. He looked like a bloody shadow, skinny as a bean. Bloody 'ell, he looked older than me. He is older than me.

Liz It wa' good, though.

Jack He ought to pack it in.

Liz That was the best bit, when it started snowing.

Jack Oh, bloody 'ell!

Liz Somebody must've left a skylight open int roof.

Jack Talk about laugh.

Liz I had to have a little titter to myself. Can you remember? He was up there singing . . . what is it? 'My Desert is Waiting', that's it, and they're all in Arab stuff, supposed to be in the desert and that, and there's all this snow that starts blowing in. I had to laugh. Best thing about it wa' that everybody wa' just ignoring it.

Jack *Desert* bloody *Song*, int middle of soddin'

December.

Liz   I enjoyed it, though. Oh, but I did have to laugh.

Jack   Aye, he ought to pack it in did John Hanson. They get money for nowt some of 'em. Money for nowt. They're good for a couple of years and then they just go on and bloody on. Same as Mario, he wa' good but it all went to his head. Mind you, Bing wa' all right, he wa' . . .

Liz   He was supposed to be fat in *The Great Caruso*, anyway.

Jack   Who?

Liz   Mario, in *The Great Caruso*, he was fat, supposed to be.

Jack   I know, Liz. I've seen it five times.

Liz   And it was Edmund Purdom who spoke the words. A smart fella wa' Edmund Purdom.

Jack   It wa' t' only film he made.

Liz   I once saw John Hanson as the Student Prince.

Jack   Blackpool.

Liz   Aye, it wa' Blackpool. Winter Gardens.

Jack   Can you remember?

Liz   I can now.

Jack   Four pounds it cost us. We'd seen it a bloody dozen times, even then. I'll never know why you wanted to see it again.

Liz   Four pounds and we had these seats behind a big pillar, can you remember? And we both had to lean to each side all the way through. It wa' a laugh, though.

Jack   It wa' a laugh. I couldn't hold me head up straight for a fortnight.

Liz   I just sat and listened after a bit. I like to sit and listen. He was good in that was John Hanson.

Jack   Aye, he was.

Liz   Put another record on, Jacko.

Jack   Who?

Liz   Put Mario on again. I like to sit and listen to Mario.

Jack   Tha' can't lick Mario.

Jack *goes to the gramophone and the lights fade. Both the actors freeze until the lights are off. A small extract of music is played.*

White light.

Jack   Scene two. Page eleven. They are both fifty.

Liz   The Munroes had an unparalleled ability for argument.

Jack   Not logical cohesive argument, just argument.

Liz   The Munroes' kitchen.

Jack   Jack is stood in front of the fire.

A spotlight cuts out the two actors.

Liz   Are you warm?

Jack   Yeh.

Liz   Why don't you shift?

Jack   Why?

Liz   Shift and let some heat come out.

Jack   I'm cold.

Liz   I am.

Jack   Go in the room then and put the fire on.

Liz   It's cold in the room.

Jack   It'll not be cold if you put the fire on.

Liz   Shift, my legs are cold.

Jack   My arse's cold.

Liz   Shift out of the way and let some heat come out.

Jack   I'm not.

Liz   Bloody shift.

Jack   I'm gerrin' warm.

Liz   You're like a big kid.

Jack   You are when you can't get your own way.

Liz   Shit, Jack.

Jack   And you shit an' all.

Blackout.

The actors sit on the chairs as if they are having a meal. Lights.

Jack   What's this I've got here?

Liz   Dinner.

Jack   I know it is.

Liz   What did you ask for then?

Jack   What is it?

Liz   Lamb.

Jack   I don't like lamb.

Liz   Gerrit.

Jack   You know I don't like . . .

Liz   Gerrit eaten, and gi' up moanin'.

Jack   Where's the sirloin?

Liz   They had none.

Jack   I'm not eatin' this.

Liz   Leave it then.

Jack   Where's my steak?

Liz   Couldn't afford it.

Jack   What?

Liz   Eat that now you've gorrit.

Jack   I don't like it.

Liz   It's best lamb is that.

Jack   I'm not bothered.

Liz   It cost me nearly a pound that.

Jack   I'm not eating it.

Liz   Leave it then. I'll have it.

Jack   It's going ont fire back in a minute is this.

Liz   Yes, you do.

Jack   Bloody lamb. Bloody lamb!

Liz   I've eaten mine.

Jack   You can shit, you can.

Liz   And you can.

Blackout.

Jack *is seated.* **Liz** *is standing.*

Liz   I've had to get up, have I?

Jack   What are you on about?

Liz   You know that I'm badly.

Jack   What have you got up for then?

Liz   Well, I didn't hear much action down here.

Jack I thought you said you weren't well.

Liz I'm not.

Jack Well, go back to bed then.

Liz I can't.

Jack Why?

Liz I can't trust you to clean up properly.

Jack Liz, just go back to bloody bed.

Liz Well, what have you done? You've been up an hour and I've not heard any movement down here yet.

Jack I've been taking the ashes out . . .

Liz And you've made a mess and all . . . look at it . . .

Jack Liz.

Liz It's no good, I'll have to do it myself.

Jack You won't. I'll get everything done. You get back up them stairs.

Liz I ask you to have a day off and you can't be bothered to help me. I'll have to do it.

Jack Listen, why don't you leave the bloody housework? It'll be here when you aren't.

Liz You know I have a good clean on Wednesdays. Have you done the brasses?

Jack Not yet.

Liz Well, what you been doing?

Jack I've had a wash, cleaned my teeth, and taken the bloody ashes out and I've had a shit. Is there anything else that you want to know?

Liz You make me bloody sick, you do.

Jack Do I?

Liz I've got the step to do. I've got the lino to wash down.

Jack Why don't you leave it for today?

Liz Coz I thought you were going to give me a hand.

Jack Jesus Christ. I've had a day off work to help you, woman, and . . . and you can do it your bloody self. I'm going out. Where's my coat?

Liz Yes, you go out and you'll never come back in here again.

Jack We'll see.

Liz Yes, we will bloody see.

Jack You're bloody house mad.

Liz I'll bloody swing for you, Jack. Look at me hands, look at my bloody arthritis.

Jack I'm bloody off to work. I'm not staying here. I don't get this at t' pit.

Jack *exits.* **Liz** *picks up a cloth.*

Liz You foul fella, you're not coming back in this house.

Liz *begins to cry and begins to wipe the stage floor. She is still crying when* **Jack** *returns.*

Jack ˉ Come here, give us that cloth.

Liz No.

Jack Give us it.

Liz No, I'll do it.

Jack I'll bloody well do it.

Liz Get off me, don't touch me . . .

Jack I'll go.

Liz Don't touch me or I'll stab you.

Jack You daft old sod ... Come here ...

He takes the cloth.

Liz Oh, you foul fella ...

Jack Put kettle on ... get a cuppa tea and go lay down.

Liz Jack, I hate you sometimes.

Jack Only sometimes? I must be getting soft in my old age.

They share a laugh through tears.

Liz You bloody thing.

Blackout.

Both actors sit in chairs and face the audience.

Liz It makes me wonder which is for the best. It gives me the creeps thinking about it.

Jack Makes little difference. Tha'll not know owt about it when it comes.

Liz It's deciding though, isn't it?

Jack It's same whatever you do.

Liz You wonder though, don't you?

Jack I don't want any flowers sendin'. I'll have 'em now.

Liz Jack, don't be so crude.

Jack They can do what they want to me. Put me in a bag and leave me int garden, or chuck me int dyke.

Liz Jack!

Jack I'll not know owt about it.

Liz You're a bloody animal.

Jack That's what they do with animals.

Liz I've never liked cremation.

Jack Nor me. I've seen enough coal being burnt.

Liz We've got five hundred int Halifax. That should take care if sommat happens.

Jack If. What're you on about *if*? There's no 'if' about it.

Liz It gives me the creeps thinking about it.

Jack Well, I only hope that it's me that goes first. Coz if it's you I've bloody had it by meself.

Liz Well, that's lovely, that is.

Jack I couldn't live without you, Liz.

Liz How do you think I'd get on without you?

Blackout.

Lights. **Liz** *is sitting.* **Jack** *has turned away from the audience.*

Liz What're you doing?

Jack Shhh!

Liz Are we going to our Betty's or what?

Jack Hang on . . . nearly finished it . . .

Liz What're you bloody doing?

Jack Writing . . .

Liz Bloody hell.

Jack A poem about t' house.

Liz Let's have a look, then.

Jack No.

Liz Come on, let's have a look.

Jack   No, gi' up.

Liz   I bet it's rubbish.

Jack   I'll read it to you.

Liz   That's like a big kid.

Jack   Right, listen . . .

Liz   Hurry up then, coz we're already late.

Jack   It's about all t' things we've had int house, you know, right . . .

A telephone table,
A lampshade blue . . .

Liz   We've only just got that telephone table, Jack.

Jack   I know.

Liz   What are you starting off with that for?

Jack   Are you going to listen or what?

Liz   Hurry up then.

Jack   And don't be bloody interfering wi' my poem . . . (*Begins in earnest.*)

A telephone table,
A lampshade blue,
A pack of cards,
Two fireguards,
A picture from a zoo,
A miner's lamp,
A cushion slightly worn,
A chandelier,
A three-speed gear,
A brass and copper horn,
An old school bell,
An elephant with a broken leg,
A plastic rose,
A plant that grows,

A gypsy doll named Peg,
An imitation oil lamp,
A purple dressing-gown,
A mirror, cracked,
A paper-rack,
A Paisley eiderdown,
A reproduction Dovaston, a poker like a sword,
A scuttle of coal, a goldfish bowl, a statue of our
    Lord,
Add many years of happiness, the right amount of
    love,
A few fears,
The same tears,
Trust in up above,
A thirty-year-old council house,
A husband
And a wife . . .
A family spent . . .
They represent
Years of married life.

A silence. **Jack** *and* **Liz** *look at each other.*

Liz   It's good.

Jack   Ar.

Liz   It is.

Jack   Ar, it's nowt. Daft, in't it?

Liz   Why don't you send it off to somebody?

Jack   Like who?

Liz   Somebody.

Jack   Ar, it's nowt. It's only a poem.

Blackout.

Jack *stands over a chair shaving:* **Liz** *comes to him.*

Liz   Have you been to look at what they've done,

next bloody door?

Jack　What?

Liz　Have you seen what them snipe-nose pigs have gone and bloody done next door? It looks an eyesore, it does.

Jack　What's up now?

Liz　Next door. I'm not kidding, it used to be all right round here, but it's a tip. You save up, you save up and buy your own bloody house and it gets worse. Have you seen what they've done? Of all the bloody lousy rotten tricks. Cut all the soddin' privets down.

Jack　So what?

Liz　Well, just look at it. They didn't want touchin'. It was just nice and private in our backs, and they've cut the buggers down.

Jack　So?

Liz　So I want something doin' about it.

Jack　But listen, love . . .

Liz　No, you're not talking me out of it.

Jack　Just listen . . .

Liz　Jack, I've had e-bloody-nough.

Jack　Will you bloody listen!

Liz　What?

Jack　Liz, they are not our privets.

Liz　They're on our part.

Jack　They are not.

Liz　Jack, some of them privets are on our part.

Jack　Well, even if they are . . .

Liz They are our bloody privets.

Jack Look, just settle down. You're gerrin' all worked up over some bleedin' privets.

Liz Do you know, you never back me up with anything, do you? I always have to battle it meself, ball comin' in t' garden, paper lad cuttin' through hedges.

Jack What is it that you want me to do?

Liz I want you to back me up.

Jack Right. Yes, it looks a bugger with them privets cut down, I agree with you.

Liz Swine.

Jack Look, Lizzy, they are their privets. If they want to cut them down they can, if they want to grow them they can, if they want to burn all the bloody lot and stick the ashes up their soddin' arse they can.

Liz Shit you.

Jack Liz, be reasonable.

Liz Shit.

Jack You shit and all.

Liz We've paid for this house and you're not bothered, are you?

Jack Course, I'm bothered. What d'you want me to do?

Liz Go round and tell 'em.

Jack Tell 'em what?

Liz Shit, Jack, just shit.

Jack For Jesus Christ's sake be bloody reasonable, woman.

Blackout.

A tight spotlight picks up **Liz**. **Jack** *stands behind her. Faces only.*

Liz   I used to be all right, no troubles, no worries. I never got depressed or fed up about my life. It was our Pam who started it. She wouldn't eat when she was younger. She'd just sit there, staring, not touching her food. I thought she'd die. She wa' that thin. She has bad asthma, she's so frail. Jack's so big and she's so thin and weak. I can't understand it. I didn't need the tablets to begin with. The more it's gone on the more I need them. I get all flustered, all worked up. I need them to calm me, to comfort me, to control me . . .

Jack   Tek a tablet.

Liz   I get depressed. I get fed up of it, the routine, the house, these four walls. This is my world in here. Like a prisoner in solitary. I never see anyone, or talk to anyone, just listen to the wireless, all day long, I'm stuck in this bloody house listening to the soddin' wireless. I'm a prisoner, Jack, in this house.

Jack   Get yourself out.

Liz   I have these funny dos.

Jack   Get yourself out.

Liz   I feel dizzy.

Jack   Have a walk to the shops.

Liz   Jack, I feel badly.

Jack   Get out more often.

Liz   I feel as dizzy as a goof.

Jack   What?

Liz   Nobody knows how I feel. I come over all dizzy. I feel like fainting, but I just go a bit groggy. I get

these bloody headaches, and pains in my stomach. I'm
in t' change. I get migraines, I'll be getting all ready to
go out shopping and I'll get a migraine. I get it so bad
that I can't see. I have to lie down. My head throbs
and my neck. I feel as if I'm going to die.

Jack   Tek a bloody tablet.

Liz   My fingers are killing me. Look at 'em, all bent
and twisted. That's with having my hands in water.
Every morning I pull the washer out. I wash every
morning. He has clean on every day – socks, trousers,
vest, underpants – every day.

Jack   They're not mucky.

Liz   Every day I clean this house from kitchen to
bedroom, from cellar to attic. All the ledges and
cupboards and carpets need cleaning. While I'm
cleaning, the washing's drying on the line, or if it's a
bad day I have to dry 'em around the fire, and then
when it's dry I iron it, and then I watch telly and then
it's bedtime and then I tek a tablet because I can't
sleep. My mind's all active.

Jack   Go to sleep, Liz.

Liz   What is there for me?

Jack   What is there for me?

Liz   What has there been in my bloody life? I've
never been out of this house. I've never been abroad,
to France or Spain or anywhere. London I went to
once, years ago. I've been to Leeds shopping and that's
it. I've been inside all the time, out of the way. It's too
late now to start to complain.

Jack   Shuttit.

Liz   What have I got to look forward to? The house,
the routine?

Jack   What about my life?

Liz   I might as well be dead. I might as well be bloody dead.

Jack   Tek a tablet, Liz.

Blackout.

Lights.

Liz   He gets me all churned up.

Jack   I don't.

Liz   If they're playing with the ball outside, or if the kids are making a noise, he's up at the bloody window looking.

Jack   You never know what they're up to.

Liz   He can't relax, he can't sit still. He's on the bloody move all the time. He's like a cat on hot bricks.

Jack   I'm not.

Liz   He'll end up in Charlie Fox's sooner than he thinks.

Jack   Undertaker's.

Liz   He will.

Jack   I'm rate.

Liz   He's allus bloody arguing, wanting to hit somebody.

Jack   I'm past that now.

Liz   He's a bloody liar. On Mischief Night they were throwing eggs at our window.

Jack   I ask you, bloody kids chucking eggs, they must have money to burn.

Liz   Jack went out to see 'em . . .

Jack *goes out to the kids.*

Jack   Oi, bugger off! Go play down your own end.
You cheeky sods.

Liz   They gave him a mouthful.

Jack   Bloody kids. I'll tell your father.

Liz (*as kids*)   He'll not do owt.

Jack   We'll see.

Liz   Jack went down the street to see their dad, Taffy
Jones.

Jack   I'd never liked him. (*Walks around the stage.*) Are
you there, Mr Jones?

Liz (*as Taff*)   Aye.

Jack   Ar, well, I've had a bit of a do with your lads.

Liz   How do you know they were my lads?

Jack   Cos I saw 'em. They've been doing mischief.

Liz   Well, it is Mischief Night.

Jack   Ar, I know, but they've been throwing eggs at
our windows. Our lass's been cleaning them all day. I
mean, it's not fair.

Liz   Well, what do you want me to do about it?

Jack   Well, if you could have a word with 'em, I
mean, I tried to talk to 'em but I got nowt but abuse
of 'em.

Liz   My kids do what they want down this street.

Jack   Well, it's not fair, is it?

Liz   They do what they want.

Jack   Could you have a word with 'em?

Liz   No, I bloody can't. They're only kids, what's up
wi' yer?

Jack   Well, if I see the buggers I'll give 'em what for.

Liz   You'll leave your hands off my kids or I'll bloody have you.

Jack   You'll what?

Liz   I'll have you.

Jack   You little worm. I'll knock your bloody head off.

Liz   And he did.

Jack   Straight over their coal bunker.

Liz   Taffy was thirty-seven.

Jack   Jack was in his fifties.

Liz   Taffy Jones went to the police station to report Jack, but the police just laughed at him.

Jack   But, I mean, chucking eggs, when you're proud of your house. It's not fair, is it? Our kids never did owt like that.

Liz   We brought them up proper.

Jack   And if they had done I'd've gi'd 'em a good hiding.

Liz   Our kids wouldn't've got caught, Jack.

A beat.

Jack   Ar, you're rate theer, crafty sods. I don't know where they got it from.

Liz   Every year when the kids were young we went to Blackpool. We went to Blackpool for fifteen years on the trot. We all loved Blackpool, me, Jack and the kids, loved it. The Golden Mile, it was different then. Winter Gardens. The Tower. Blackpool changed, everything changes. Then we went to Cleethorpes and then to Whitley Bay.

Jack It's nice and quiet.

Liz We started in a big posh hotel at Blackpool on honeymoon on the sea front, then we went to a little guest house down Waterloo Road, and then a bed-and-breakfast near the Coliseum bus station and now in a caravan at Whitley Bay.

Jack Nice and quiet.

Liz My nerves get bad, they get bloody awful. We have a week a year to get away from it.

Jack It's grand to get away.

Liz From the house.

Jack From the pit.

Liz From the routine.

Jack And the muck.

Liz From the soddin' washing.

Jack Soddin' arguments.

Liz My nerves are bad, bloody awful. Before we ever go away I get all upset, even when I'm packing the cases. I get nervous, being on the road and all that. I enjoy it when I'm there. I wish to Christ we could afford more time away. When I'm there, when I'm away from home, I don't ever want to come back.

Blackout.

White lights up.

Jack Page twenty. Whitley Bay. The Schooner Nightclub.

Liz A large wooden shell of a building with a large audience.

Jack It is the last night of their annual holiday.

Liz The Munroes demonstrated little . . .

Jack   If any . . .

Liz   . . . exhibitionism. Their barometer of enjoyment
was permanently frozen up. However, Liz would allow
herself, once a year, a few brandy and limes, a bag of
crisps, a foxtrot, a Broadway quickstep . . .

Jack   A saunter together . . .

Liz   . . . and she was well on her way to a good night
out. She even learnt sequence dancing especially for
this week's holiday. On the Friday night of the week's
holiday the caravan site would celebrate with a . . .

Jack   'Mr and Mrs' competition.

Liz   Jack was a reluctant entrant, but Liz loved it.

Music. Lights.

Jack   In this scene I play a typical site-club compère.

Liz   And I play a slightly inebriated Elizabeth
Munroe.

Jack (*as compère*)   Right. Sh sh, listen, be quiet at the
back. Listen, be quiet, my dad's in bed. Sh! Right
then. Now, you know what we've done. We've sent her
husband into the sound-proof box. Well, to be honest,
the lovely Adele takes them out through this door and
into the car round the back. And they sit with the car
radio on, but anyway. Now then, now then, we have
here, Elizabeth.

Liz   Yes, that's right.

Jack   Are you enjoying it here?

Liz   Yeh, it's smashin'. We allus come every year.

Jack   Great, that's what we like to hear, my love.
Now then, are you here for a fortnight?

Liz   No, we're going back tomorrow.

Jack   Oh shame, never mind, my love, I bet you'll be

back next year?

Liz   Hope so.

Jack   And we hope so as well, Elizabeth, we do. Can I call you Liz?

Liz   Yes, you can call me what you want.

Jack   Now then, Liz, now then. Doesn't she laugh a lot! Look at her laughing! Are you shy? Ohhh! She's shy, aren't you? Now then, listen, this is not hard. You know what to do, don't you?

Liz   Yeh.

Jack   Have you got anybody out there?

Liz   No.

Jack   Any family?

Liz   Daughter and a son.

Jack   Lovely, are they grown up?

Liz   Yeh.

Jack   Lovely, smashin'. Right then, now then. You know what the idea of the game is. I'm going to ask you what did your husband, Jack . . . is it Jack?

Liz   Yeh.

Jack   What did your husband Jack say that *you'd* say to these questions? You get a point for each correct answer and a tenner for all three correct. Is that clear?

Liz   Yes, I know what to do.

Jack   I'm glad somebody knows what's going on. Right then, are you ready? Right, this is your first question. I asked Jack: 'If you had to travel somewhere on holiday, let's say abroad, how would you want to travel? By train, by car, by bus? How would you travel: car, bus or train? Think carefully. What did

Jack say that you would prefer to do – car, bus, train?

Liz   I think he'd say, bus.

Jack   *Yes*. Well done, my love, well done. That's one out of one. Are you going away again this year?

Liz   No, no, we're not.

Jack   Shame. Anyway, now then, one out of one, not bad, not bad at all. Right then, second question. I asked Jack. What is the last item of clothing that you take off before you get ready for bed? What did your Jack say was the last item?

Liz   D'you mean before I put my nightie on?

Jack   Yes, my lovely, yes. What did he say?

Liz   Ohhh! I daren't say it.

Jack   She says she daren't say it. What is it that you wear?

Liz   My whatsit.

Jack   'My whatsit'?

Liz   Bra, brassière.

Jack   Is exactly what he said, my love, exactly. Well done, Liz, my love. That's great, really great. Two out of two, smashin'. Right then, now then, last one. Are you ready?

Liz   Yes.

Jack   Last one. Take your time and think very carefully. Do you keep bits of paper in the house? After you've unwrapped something, a present or anything, do you keep, do you keep the paper. Think carefully what did Jack say. Do you keep them, yes or no?

Liz   Yes, I keep everything tidy.

Jack Liz. That is exactly what he said. Well done. My lovely Adele, bring Jack out of the car. Elizabeth you have just won for you and your husband a ten-pound note, and a bottle of champagne.

Liz Whoooo!

Jack Whoooo! She says. A bottle of champers. Well done, my love, well done. Give her a big hand, everybody.

Blackout.

Jack *goes and changes his costume at the hat-stand.* **Liz** *stands still. She brings a chair downstage, stands behind it.*

Liz During the afternoon Jack and Liz would have a steady walk down to St Mary's lighthouse.

Jack *is taking off his coat.*

Jack They would stand and watch the tide come in, covering up the road to the lighthouse.

Liz In this scene, it is dusk.

Jack Both of them are leaning over the railings, you know, as people do.

The chairs have been turned in such a way as to resemble prom railings. Both **Jack** *and* **Liz** *lean over. The lights slightly dim.*

Liz Eee, I love it, Jack.

Jack I do.

Liz Blackpool wa' nice, but . . .

Jack Well, it's quieter.

Liz I've always liked up North East.

Jack I have.

Liz I've never been on a boat, Jack.

Jack No, I haven't.

Liz Can you remember when we went paddling at Blackpool?

Jack I can. We've had many a happy hour paddling.

Liz And I couldn't stop sneezing that night, could I?

Jack Water wa' like ice.

Liz Can you remember seeing *Gigi*?

Jack Ar.

Liz One of my favourites.

Jack Ar.

Liz What did he say?

Jack Who?

Liz Maurice ... Chevalier, when they're sat by the sea ...

Jack Oh, ar. I can remember. Ar, did it go ...

Liz *begins to sing.*

Liz
We dined alone.
We dined with friends.
A tenor sang ...

Jack No, no, that's not rate ...

Liz That's it, Jack.

Jack Is it, hell. I can remember it as if it were yesterday ... (*As Chevalier.*) We met at nine.

Liz We met at eight.

Jack I was on time.

Liz You were late.

Jack Oh, yes, I remember it well.

Liz We dined with friends.

Jack That's it.

Liz We dined alone.

Jack A tenor sang.

Liz A baritone.

Jack Oh, yes, I remember it well. The dazzling April moon.

Liz There was none that night. And the month was June.

Both That's right, that's right.

Liz
It warms my heart to know
That you remember still,
The way you do . . .

Jack Oh, yes. I remember it well.

Liz Then they talk for a bit.

Jack He talks because she's just sat listening.

Liz She talked funny, didn't she?

Jack Well, they wa' French.

Liz No, I didn't mean that.

Jack That carriage ride.

Liz You walked me home.

Jack You lost a glove.

Liz I lost a comb.

Jack
Oh, yes, I remember it well.
That brilliant sky.

Liz We had some rain.

Jack Those Russian songs.

Both   From sunny Spain?

Jack
Oh, yes, I remember it well.
You wore a gown of gold.

Liz   I was all in blue.

Jack (*stops. A beat*)   Am I getting old?

Liz (*looks*)
Oh no, not you,
How strong you were,
How young and gay,
A prince of love,
In every way.

Jack   Oh, yes, I remember it well.

Blackout.

Lights.

Liz   It's a nice house. It's warm. It gets bloody lonely.
When you're by yourself for a long time in the same
house, in the same rooms, you start to think about
things. You can't help it. Ideas take over your mind,
become massive, uncontrollable. Something that's been
said, the smallest words that have been said take on
more and more significance. They keep ringing in your
head, getting louder and louder. It's like if Jack's home
late from the pit. I imagine things that might happen
to him. I can't help it. He may have had a car crash.
His driving's getting worse. Maybe there's been an
accident at the pit. There's a lot of accidents.
Sometimes I've thought that he might be seeing
another woman. I get all churned up inside. Or I think
that he's fighting again. I mean, you don't know where
he is, do you? Two miles under the ground, that's a
long way away, a long way. It's funny, you wouldn't
think it about Jack, but he's a kind bloke. We fall out,
we argue, I call him all the lousy names under the

sun, but he'd do owt for me. I never show him any
affection but, you know? I used to. I used to love him
physically, I mean really love him. I wa' proud of him
being a big ignorant fella, a tough nut, not-give-a-
damn attitude. When we were younger in bed it wa'
like sleeping with a mountain, sleeping at the side of a
mountain. I wa' snug and asleep in the valley and Jack
wa' the mountain keeping the cold and wind off me,
keeping me warm and safe. I thought that if he's here
I'm not scared of dying, and that's what I'm most
frightened of. I'm not allus right to him. It takes a lot.
I waste all my time doing other things, cleaning the
house, occupying my mind. When it comes to the
important things like sitting down together, taking time
over each other, I haven't got the energy. I don't feel
like doing it. I just take him for granted. He keeps on
going to work and I assume that everything's OK. I
know it's not the best way to run things, but in this life
we just go on. Things affect us, but me? I just keep
going.

You wouldn't believe me if I told you that Jack wa'
soft. He is, as soft as a brush. When our Ian wa' born
the nurse asked him if he wanted to come and see the
birth. He nearly fainted. I nearly died. He stood
outside in the corridor, writing a poem. What a sight,
a bloke the size of Jack scribbling a poem on a bit of
envelope. The poem was about the pit, not me. He
said that he just wanted to write about the pit, how
proud he was, just how proud he was. He's still got
that poem somewhere in the house. I think he's written
one or two, all about the pits. He's as soft as a brush.

I go in hospital. I wanted to tell you, I've been
meaning to tell you this last five minutes. I go in on
Wednesday. I've had some tests. It's been coming this
has for years. I've got an ulcer. I think it's a growth.
As I said, you think about a lot of things when you're
by yourself. I imagine this thing inside me. It's awful.

It's in my womb. I asked the doctor, 'Is it malignant?' He said, 'No.' But you're never satisfied, are you? . . . I'll need that week's holiday when I come out. It's not that I'm worrying about going in. Once you've had kids you're not bothered about much. It's just that I wish I'd been in and come out. I wish, I wish to God it was all over and done with and I wa' back here in this house, my home.

Lights fade.

Act Two

White light. **Jack** *and* **Liz** *are putting the chairs together to make a sort of bath seat. They do this through* **Jack***'s speech.*

Jack Jack really paid little attention to his son Ian, especially when he was in his infancy. It wasn't until Ian was sixteen that Jack discovered how quickly he'd grown up, and how little actual time he had spent with his son.

Liz Consequently when Ian married and had a son, Jack assumed it as his own. The child would stay with his grandad for weekend after weekend. Jack made him a hut, and a tree-house and a barrow to help in the garden.

Jack The child loved it.

Liz Particularly when his grandad gave him his Satd'y night bath.

Jack Page thirty-five. The bathroom at Saxon Terrace.

Liz The walls are emulsioned, the floor covered with oilcloth.

Jack Jack has the task of bathing his grandson.

Liz In this scene I play an 'unlikely' grandson.

Jack And I play a very contented 'Happy Jack'.

They are 'in' the situation.

Liz (*as grandson*) *More water!* Grandad, more water.

Jack You know what yer gran's said.

Liz Come on.

Jack Look out. Let me get these sleeves rolled up and we'll gi' thee a wesh.

Liz   Don't splash us.

Jack   Dun't splash thee, dun't splash thee. Dun't tha want to be hard like thee grandad?

Liz   Yeh.

Jack   Put thee muscle up and let's have a look at it.

Liz   I 'ant got any muscle.

Jack   Thy has, let's have a look. Oh, ar! It's theer, it's comin' on is that.

Liz   Is it?

Jack   Like knots in cotton.

Liz   Can we have some more water in? I'm freezin'.

Jack   Aye, we can do, but dun't tell thee gran. If she finds out that I'm running off her hot water, she'll play 'ell wi' me. Theer, is that enough?

Liz   Yeh, it's warm.

Jack   It wants to be.

Liz   Tell us a tale, Grandad.

Jack   No, I'm busy weshin' thee.

Liz   Tell us a tale.

Jack   I've teld thee 'um all.

Liz   Tell us one agen, Grandad, tell us one.

Jack   Which one? I've got that many.

Liz   Tell us about when you nearly got picked to play football for England.

Jack   No, I'm not tellin' thee that 'un. I get shown up.

Liz   Tell us about when you wa' in Africa.

Jack   No, look, I'm not tellin' thee one. Tha's heard

too many stories thy has.

Liz Tell us one.

Jack Bloody no! And that's swearin', now be teld.

Liz Tell us.

Jack No.

Liz Tell us, Grandad. I love thee.

Jack How much?

Liz (*making a sign*) About that much.

Jack That's not much.

Liz Tell us.

Jack No.

Liz Right then. I'm tellin' me gran.

Jack What?

Liz You've let me have some more water in an' she said I could only have a drop in. And then she'll shout at yer, and you swore at me. You called me bloody, and she'll shout at yer for that when I tell her.

Jack When did I swear?

Liz You called me 'bloody'.

Jack You little sod.

Liz (*shouting*) Gran! Me grandad's just swored at me.

Jack Sh, sh, you little bugger.

Liz You bugger, you bugger.

Jack I'll tell thee sommat that I've never teld anybody else int world.

Liz What?

Jack When I ran away.

Liz   Did you run away?

Jack   Yeh. I ran away to a circus.

Liz   When?

Jack   Whooo! When I was as old as you. One day I left me mam and dad and I caught a bus and I ran away to a circus and London.

Liz   What for?

Jack   Sommat to do, adventure.

Liz   Wa' it good?

Jack   Great. I was the youngest lion-tamer in the world. I'd be put in the ring wi' this lion, and it'd look at me, and I'd look at it, and then I'd grab it by its fur, all its fur round its neck, an' I'd pick it up wi' me muscles, and I'd swing it. Round me head. An' when I thought that it wa' dizzy enough, I'd let it go.

Liz   What did it do, Grandad?

Jack   It tried to stand up, and it looked at me and then it walked off, a bit dodgy and told all them other lions to look out for me. An' all crowd wa' clappin' an' goin' mad, an' chuckin' money. An' these lions would do owt I teld 'um.

Liz   What did you used to seh to 'um?

Jack   I'd seh, 'Ungowa. Get in that cage.'

Liz   How long did you be a lion-tamer for?

Jack   Only a week, an' then I came back because I was hungry. It's not right good pay being a lion-tamer.

Liz   What about all that money that they chucked at yer?

Jack   What money?

Liz You said that they all went mad an' chucked money.

Jack Oh, yeh, that money. Ohh I, er, had to give it to the bloke in charge, an' that. Anyway I had to come back because I missed my schooling.

Liz Urgh! School.

Jack What's up?

Liz School stinks of baba.

Jack Na' then.

Liz Did you go to school then, Grandad?

Jack Once or twice, nip, once or twice. Do you want some more hot water?

Blackout.

Liz *remains where she is.* **Jack** *goes to the hat-stand. In the dark we hear screaming. (A spotlight on* **Jack**. **Liz** *maybe remains.)*

Jack Ar, once or twice, it's rate an' all is that bugger. I never put much store by book learning, didn't seem to make much sense to me. I've got two hands, and I can handle a shovel, and I know how coal gets made. That's about the sum total of my schooling. Mind you, I can print really well. That's all I can remember from school, having to print out letters all the bloody time. I've learnt this much: if you want owt, you've got to work for it, nobody's gonna hand it to yer on a plate. I've worked for everything we've got ... and that's not much by other standards. Before Liz had our Ian I never had a day off from the pit ... never had a laker ... I thought I was working for sommat, sommat important. Hun? I must have been bloody loose. We wa' scratin' and saving up trying to mek sommat for ussens. I never had time to see that I wa' getting older, slowing down. I'd been doing the

same amount of work at forty as I was doing at twenty
. . . ar . . . working? Working for what? For who?
National Coal Board. (*Laughs.*) I've upset some people
in my time, lad, I've upset some of the buggers.

A beat.

Don't thee be like thee grandfather. Thee go and mek
sommat of thee life. Don't thee be a bloody miner. For
God's sake, make sommat for yersen.

Blackout.

Liz   Jack! Jack! For God's sake! The lights of the
theatre were bright and warm, blinding. I was soaking
with sweat. All I can remember is that my knees were
up in the air, and I could just about see the large
hillock that was to become our Ian. The (*Screams out of
the blue.*) pain was excruciating.

Jack   Jack was stood outside. He was nervous. 'What
had I done?' he thought. I hope she's gunna be all
right. You don't think about this side of it.

Liz   She had been rushed to the hospital in an
ambulance.

Jack   Jack was twice sick in the ambulance. He felt
an urge to put some idea down on paper, all he had
was the back of an envelope. (*Writing.*) Do you ever
stop to think?

Liz   I am pushing, I'm trying my best.

Jack   Have you ever thought about a miner?

Liz   I'm trying, aren't I? I'm tryin'. (*She screams.*)

Jack   Christ! I'm glad I'm not a woman.

Liz   I am pushing. It was a difficult birth.

Jack   Have you ever stopped to wonder?

Liz (*screaming*)   Jack!

Jack
> Have you ever stopped to wonder,
> When you think about our coal,
> How a miner leaves his loved ones
> To descend the Devil's hole?

Liz It was a big baby. Like having twins.

Jack
> Have you ever stopped to wonder of inequalities in
>   life,
> How easily found underground is pain and sweat
>   and strife?
> Have you ever stopped to wonder, with your life so
>   fine,
> That a miner's education takes place deep, down a
>   mine?

Liz Ten pounds and three ounces. Liz was in great pain.

Jack Have you ever stopped to wonder?

Liz (*whispering*) Jack?

Jack Have you ever stopped to wonder?

Liz (*louder*) Jack?

Jack
> Have you ever stopped to wonder,
> When ambition they have none,
> That society has left them,
> With all ambition gone?
> Have you ever stopped to wonder
> Why they show but small respect,
> That years of exploitation
> Leaves something to suspect.

Liz It was a beautiful baby boy. Blue eyes, blond hair. She immediately called him Ian.

Jack Ian John Munroe.

Liz Liz was very ill for several days. She was to have

a blood transfusion. She almost lost her life. Ian John Munroe was four days old before Liz saw him. And Jack . . . still in the corridor.

Jack Have you ever stopped to wonder?

Liz *stands besides* **Jack**.

Liz Why I'm on the miners' side?

Both
We were born beneath a muck stack
And we speak of it with pride.

Lighting change.

Jack Page forty-one. The honeymoon. It was the week of the St Leger when they decided to take their honeymoon. Four days at Blackpool. They stopped in the Metropole on the sea front near the north pier. Liz had always wanted to stop at the Metropole. It was a dream come true.

Liz Those four days were full of mixed emotions, for both of them. Seeing Jack away from the pit was like seeing a fish out of water. They spent most of the time looking around the shops, walking on the pier and keeping out of the rain. One evening they paid to see Reginald Dixon play the organ in the Tower Ballroom.

The actors have proceeded to set up the Tower Ballroom.

Jack It happened like this. I wanted to see Reginald Dixon. I had always admired his playing. It was raining so we decided that a few hours in the Tower Ballroom would be a good idea. I was shocked at the price, two and six, but it was my honeymoon so I thought, sod it! This big commissionaire fella took me and Liz and about twenty more people to this room, opened the door, in we went, then he shut the door. About ten minutes later organ music started to seep into the room. (*Reginald Dixon: 'Begin the Beguine'.*) The noise wa' comin' through speakers in the wall.

Everybody looked amazed, but no one said a word.
We'd all paid to *see* Reg play and we were in a room
listening to him.

Liz   For about ten minutes no one spoke or looked at
each other, then Jack said.

Jack   Hold on a minute, we're not havin' this.

Liz   And he left the room telling everyone else to . . .

Jack   Wait theer!

Liz   He went up to the woman behind the box office.

Jack   Excuse me, love. Can you tell me where the
commissionaire is?

Liz *has become the woman behind the till.*

Liz   I'm sorry, love, but he's not here.

Jack   Where is he, love?

Liz   I don't know, love.

Jack   Well, what's the game, love?

Liz   What d'you mean?

Jack   I mean, what's game here? We've paid five bob
to see Reg Dixon and we're stuck in a soddin' chicken
box listening to him.

Liz   Well, you see . . .

Jack   If I'd've wanted to listen to him, I'd've bought
his records.

Liz   Well, what d'you want me to do?

Jack   I want to know why we're in theer.

Liz   Well you see the BBC are recording him today.

Jack   Tha what? And you've got twenty people in a
soddin' box?

Liz   It's not my idea.

Jack   Whose idea is it?

Liz   I don't know.

Jack   I want my money back.

Liz   I'm sorry, sir, but we can't give you a refund.

Jack   Tha what!

Liz   I'm afraid we can't refund.

Jack   D'you mean to tell me that you've willingly took me money and made us listen to someb'dy coz soddin' BBC's recording? Well, I'll tell you sommat. You couldn't run a bloody raffle. Get me the bloody manager, and get him me quick.

Liz   There's no need to shout at me. You know I'm only doing my job.

Jack   I know it's not your fault, love, but isn't it all right, eh?

Liz   You know, I don't think that the manager will see you.

Jack   Well you'd better go and try an' get him, love, or I'll pull you through that soddin' grille . . . The manager came, and Jack got his money back. In fact all twenty or so got their money back. The manager wasn't pleased, but there was little he could do.

Liz   In those days Jack really wasn't bothered about anyone. No matter what position they held he would hold them with the same ignorant, arrogant disregard, as he said . . .

Jack   Even t' Queen Mother shits. She's no different to me.

Liz   Two days later in the Manchester Hotel, a large pub at the corner of Lytham Road, the barman had

short-changed Jack of threepence. The barman was an
enormously fat arrogant Lancastrian. I thought that
Jacko had met his match.

Liz *is behind a chair washing glasses.*

Jack   Oi.

Liz (*as barman*)   Oi what?

Jack   Oi, can I have a word?

Liz   Tha'll get more than a word.

Jack   Oh, aye?

Liz   Yeh!

Jack   Tha wants to lose some weight before tha starts
threatenin'.

Liz   Tha wants to learn to talk before tha starts
arguing.

Jack (*to the audience*)   Jack gave him one of his heavy
depressed and dangerous looks. (*He does so.*)

Liz (*changing approach*)   What's up?

Jack   I'll tell thee what's up. I'm threepence short.

Liz   You what?

Jack   Tha's short-changed me of threepence.

Liz   Give over.

Jack   Aye up. I'm tellin' thee, tha's short-changed me.

Liz   I 'aven't.

Jack   Thy has. I've just reckoned it up.

Liz   Right, what did you have?

Jack   Never mind what I had, just gimme me money.

Liz   Look, pal . . .

Jack Don't 'look pal' me, pal. Tha's done me for threepence. Na' is th' gunna give it me or what?

Liz How much did you give me?

Jack That dun't matter. I've worked it out. I want threepence.

Liz Well, look . . .

Jack Thee bloody look. I'll pull thee over that soddin' bar if tha' dun't gi' me it.

Blackout.

Lights straight back up.

Liz It was a good honeymoon, Jack being so reasonable with everyone. Jack created experiences and electric situations, especially with Liz.

Jack *and* **Liz** *sit together as if eating a meal. A spotlight picks them out. They mime eating for a while.* **Jack** *eats throughout the dialogue until it is no longer possible.*

Liz It's lovely in here, isn't it?

Jack 'S all right.

Liz Good service.

Jack 'S all right.

Liz I like it.

Jack Good.

Liz Good service. He's a nice waiter. Very pleasant.

Jack Yeh, all right.

Liz I bet he's got that tan living here.

Jack Yeh.

Liz I think he's good-looking, that waiter.

Jack Ar?

Liz I think he's *sexy*.

There is a deafening silence.

Jack, I think he's attractive, that waiter.

Jack Who?

Liz Him that's been serving us.

Jack That thing that's been hovering about?

Liz He's nice.

Jack When he comes back, I'm gunna kill him.

Liz Jack?

Jack I'm gunna kill him.

Liz I only said . . .

Jack You said it. You bloody said it.

Liz I didn't mean it. I only said it to see what you'd say.

Jack He's bloody dead when he comes for the sweet orders.

Liz Please, Jack.

Jack Don't 'please Jack' me. I'm six foot of idiot jealousy. I work in a bloody hole in the ground. I'm massive. Eight hours a day in pitch black, and you say that an article like that is 'sexy'. I'd look sodding sexy working at the seaside all year. You say that he's sexy again and I'll crucify you.

A moment.

I could beat him at everything. Name one thing that he could beat me at. Jesus Christ, Liz, you've got an enormous bloke with you, who'd do everything you want, and you've got the cheek to call him sexy. He couldn't pick his pit cheque up.

A moment.

All right then, tek off. Tek off with your sexy waiter.

Liz   I don't want to.

Jack   Well, don't then.

Liz   He's like a streak of pump water anyway.

Jack   He's like a skull on a stick.

Liz   It took Liz a long time to realise that Jack's absurd jealousy was an expression of his absolute devotion. She was quite pleased when the honeymoon was over. As far as the waiter was concerned, they left after the main course without paying, before Jack had a chance to carry out his threats.

Jack   Which she knew he would.

Liz   Their wedding was a quiet but pleasant affair. Held at the local parish church. Liz was all dressed in white and Jack looked smart, if a little bit choked in his wedding suit. Everything was going very smoothly until we came to the wedding photos.

Liz *holds* **Jack** *by the arm and they smirk as if posing for a photo.*

Liz   Smile, Jack.

Jack   I am smiling.

Liz   You're not.

Jack   I can't smile, rate. It looks daft.

Liz   It doesn't. It looks nice. Smile.

Jack   Gi' up.

Liz *(whispering)*   Bloody smile.

Jack   I am.

Liz *(whispering)*   Smile more.

Jack Oh, bloody all . . . all right.

Jack *gives a big daft smile, a light flashes, and that's their wedding photo.* **Jack** *leans forward and touches* **Liz**.

Jack Jack had the undoubted ability to express himself through actions rather than words.

Liz When he was twenty he would travel thirty miles every other weekend to see Liz, who was in 'service' for Wilsons Mill Firm in Bradford. He would collect her from her digs, and they would walk around the city, looking in the shop windows, thinking of what to buy, though they never bought anything. In the late afternoon they would go to the cinema.

Jack In the next scene Jack gives Liz her first ever present.

Liz A quarter-pound of coconut mushrooms.

Jack They would go to the Gaumont no matter what was showing.

During the last dialogue the actors have put the chairs together facing the audience. They then go and stand upstage left. They open a door and are blinded by the darkness. **Liz** *tries to hold on to* **Jack**, *probably by a sleeve or jacket pocket only. They hobble down an aisle, and see two seats. These seats are behind the 'real' seats. They shove their way to the seats and then decide to move to the 'real' seats. They move into the aisle once again. They reach the row of seats with the two real seats on them.* **Jack** *tells an imaginary gent,* Excuse me, pal. *We imagine him standing and both* **Liz** *and* **Jack** *squeezing past him and others to their place. They mime taking off their outside coats, which is a big job. They sit in their respective seats for a moment, getting comfortable, then* **Liz** *announces,* I can't see. **Jack**, *being the gent, decides to change seats. It is an effort to move in this confined space. Eventually they get comfortable.* **Jack** *prods an imaginary person in front of him with his hand.* Tek your feet down I can't see owt. That's better. *The two actors begin to cough in an attempt to simulate the whole of*

*the cinema. Intermittently they will turn around and tell the
'other' members of the cinema to* be quiet, shuttit! *etc. Finally
they begin to watch the film in earnest. At varying intervals*
Jack *may burst into enormous horse laughing.* **Liz** *may laugh
as well but she gives* **Jack** *scolding looks when he laughs loudly.
He may touch her leg in the most masculine manner. She looks
at him and smiles. She may touch his hand. He looks at her.*

Jack   I've bought thee sommat.

Liz   What?

Jack   Sommat tha likes. (*Turns around, answering someone
in the audience.*) Shut thee soddin' mouth or I'll have
thee head off.

Liz   Don't, Jack.

Jack   Coconut mushrooms.

Liz   Thanks, Jack.

Jack   Tha likes 'em, dun't tha?

Liz   Course I do.

Jack   Oh.

Liz   Thanks a lot.

Jack   Aren't you going to open them?

Liz   Yeh, I can do.

Jack   Give us one. (*She gives him a sweet.*)
MMMmmmm, they're nice are these, my favourites.

Liz   Liz enjoyed Jack's fortnightly visits. It was the
only time she came out of her digs. Before she went
away to Bradford they were always together. They
would often walk down Sandy Lane and sit and talk
for hours.

Jack   Liz was a never-ending revelation to Jack, her
innocence and inquisitiveness fascinated him.

They sit, as if on grass.

Liz Jack?

Jack What?

Liz Do you know what I've been thinking?

Jack If I knew that I'd be on at the City Varieties at Leeds

Liz You know when you're down the pit?

Jack Yeh . . .

Liz Where do you go?

Jack What are you on about?

Liz Well, do you come back up or do you go down there?

Jack Go where?

Liz Well . . . toilet?

Jack *laughs.*

Jack Bloody hell, woman.

Liz What's up?

Jack There's no lavs down t' pit. You have to go in a corner.

Liz Oh, bloody hell, Jack.

Jack Listen, guess where we put our snap tins.

Liz In lockers?

Jack In corners. Half t' time when you get your snap tin somebody's messed all over it.

Liz I thought you could come back up.

Jack You can . . . after eight hours.

Liz That's disgusting is that.

Jack   Ar.

Liz   It's bound to get better, Jack, in't it? You know, as years go on.

Jack   Oh, ar it's bound to get better.

Liz   On Sundays the pair of them would have a walk up to Burntwood. They would never hold hands, but Liz felt a close bond between them. Jack would often impose his poetry on Liz.

Jack   Granted, it was rough, badly written poetry. Jack had penned it during his quarter of an hour break down the pit. The paper it was written on was filthy. But they both enjoyed trying to decipher what Jack had thought in that black hole two miles deep.

Seated on chairs; overhead spotlight.

Liz
From down the mine so perilous
I heard a collier calling to us,
One clear call from the bowels of the earth,

Jack
'Pay the miner what he's worth.'

Both
'Hey there, hey there, you up there,
Pay the miner his rightful share.'

Jack
Pray for him when underground,
Exploited for the capitalist pound,
Toiling away his working hour,
Meagrely selling his labour power.

Liz
He moves to his workplace through the murk,
Where the roof is mesh and dangers lurk.
With muscles taut and a sight that's failing,
I heard a miner hailing,

Jack
    Hailing.

Both
    'Hey there hey there, you up there,
    Pay the miner his rightful share.'
    Down the mine wherein dwells death
    The collier works with hard-fought breath.
    Gleaming bodies, legs that ache,
    Sweat and strain, back fit to break.
    When danger calls they'll tighten ranks.
    They ask no pity, they ask no thanks,
    And all we ask of you up there.

Liz   Is pay the miner his rightful share.

Jack   Page sixty, the final scene.

Liz   Their first encounter.

Jack   Jack first asked Liz to 'go out' with him when they were seventeen.

Liz   Though, as we have said, they had known each other for years.

Jack   He was on his way back from the pit, taking a short cut by coming down the side of West Street.

Liz   She was in West Street Co-op, just coming out . . . Hello, Jack.

Jack   Hello, Liz. How are you?

Liz   I'm fine, thanks, Jack. How're you?

Jack   I'm all right.

Liz   Have you just finished work?

Jack   I'm on days regular. Where've you been?

Liz   I've just been in the Co-op.

Jack   Oh, yeh.

Liz   You're all dirty.

Jack   Yeh. I haven't hed time for a bath today, I'm going to the Miners' Welfare dance tonight.

Liz   Oh, I wish I could go.

Jack   Aren't you going?

Liz   No.

Jack   That's a nice dress you're wearing.

Liz   Oh, thank you.

Jack   It suits your eyes.

Liz   Does it?

Jack   Can I ask you something?

Liz   Yes, of course.

Jack   Well, it's just that, we've known each other for a long time, haven't we?

Liz   Yes, we have.

Jack   Since we were kids.

Liz   That's right.

Jack   We've always been friends and played together, all our lives.

Liz   Yes.

Jack   And I've always liked you, as a friend.

Liz   I've always liked you, Jack.

Jack   Have you?

Liz   Yes, always. You've always been a good worker, and honest. You've got broad shoulders, and you're kind.

Jack   I can't explain what I feel for you, Liz, you're the only woman in my life.

Liz   I love you, Jack.

Jack   Why don't I take you to the dance? D'you want to come?

Liz   I'd love to.

Jack   I'll nip up home and get fettled. Liz, I'm really glad that you like me.

Liz   I do.

Jack   I'll see you tonight then?

Liz   Will you call for me?

Jack   Yeh, about sevenish?

Liz   Right.

Jack   Good.

Liz   See you about sevenish then. That was actually fictional dialogue.

Jack   A dramatisation, if you like.

Liz   Pretence.

Jack   You see, it didn't happen quite like that.

Liz   Though we believe that perhaps they wished that it had.

Jack   Maybe it did happen like that in their minds.

Liz   But just to put the record straight . . .

Jack   And to deal with the facts . . .

Liz   It happened like this . . .

Liz *and* **Jack** *re-act the last scene.*

Jack   Oi.

Liz   Oi what?

Jack   Look at thee, about as much fat on a chip.

Liz   Look at theesen first – more mouth than muscle.

Jack   Tha what?

Liz   Tha wants a rate good wash.

Jack   Shut thee rattle, Elizabeth Cooper, and get your body over here.

Liz *walks to him.*

Liz   What's tha want?

Jack   What's tha doing toneet?

Liz   Nowt, why? Who's interested?

Jack   Me.

Liz   Oh, yeh?

Jack   'S tha wanna come up to t' Welfare wi' me?

Liz   Are you asking me out with you?

A beat.

Jack   Ar, I suppose so.

Liz   Well, ask me then.

A moment's hesitation.

Jack   Will tha go out wi me?

A beat.

Liz   Yeh, Jack Munroe . . . I can do.

They freeze. Steve Conway plays 'Good Luck, Good Health, God Bless You'. Costumes are taken off and placed on the chairs.

September in the Rain

September in the Rain was first presented professionally by Hull Truck Theatre Company in 1984 with the following cast:

Jack   John Godber
Liz   Jane Clifford

Directed by John Godber

Act One

As the audience enters the theatre **Jack** *and* **Liz** *are sitting among their luggage or are getting their luggage together. Ken Dodd sings. A slide of Blackpool is projected on the backcloth.* **Liz** *takes some deep breaths. They are waiting for their bus to arrive. They are in their late sixties. They are wrapped up but are not wearing raincoats.*

Liz (*to audience*) Oh. Oh, I love the sea air. Clears my head. Do you know I've allus liked Blackpool air, it's thicker in some way, there's more texture to it, you can feel it doing you good. Sommat about it refreshes me. Look at it, even in September it's smashing, even when everything's grey it warms me to be here. I could live here. I've said to Jack many a time, 'We ought to have bought a boarding house at Blackpool, made a go of it, Jack.' He's never been keen. Nowt can move him when he puts his mind to it. Too late to start to make changes now. Mind you, Blackpool's changed. It has. We've just had a last walk down Central Drive and all that's changed, and there wasn't the fancy front on Tussaud's when we first came. Or as many amusements on the Golden Mile, was there, Jack?

Jack No.

Liz We've only been here for a few days, been stopping at a guest house up north, past the Cenotaph, hope that's not an omen. It's quieter up there away from the bingo and the slots. We like it quiet now. It's a nice run to Blackpool, you know? Only takes an hour and a half on the M62. We're from Yorkshire, aren't we, Jack?

Jack Ar.

Liz We used to come here every year.

Jack Ar, we did, ar.

Liz We came to Blackpool for years. Things happen that fast I can't allus place them in the right year, if you know what I mean.

Jack I know what you mean.

Liz Jack's allus said that when he goes, they can scatter his ashes all over Blackpool sands.

Jack Bloody hell, Liz.

Liz He's not been hisself since he had a bit of a do with his heart.

Jack Bloody hell.

Liz That's why we've come ont bus, can't drive and be safe now really. But it's a lovely run with Wallace Arnold, they've got hundreds of buses, you can see them all pulling in. People from all over the place still flock to Blackpool. Hey, you mun't call Blackpool, not while me and Jack's about. You can't lick Blackpool for my money.

Jack No.

Liz I allus liked coming ont bus, Jack liked to come int car. Liked to be able to stop where he wanted. First time we came away int car, ee, it wa' a laugh. We'd got this Ford Anglia, ain't we, Jack? Green it was, green and white.

Jack Ford Popular. It was green and cream.

Liz Was it cream?

Jack Ten, twenty-seven, W Y.

Liz I'll never forget that registration number.

Jack Six hundred and fifty-eight pound cash I paid for it.

Liz I wanted to put that money down on a deposit

for a house. But you know Jack, if you tell him to do summat he just goes and does the bloody opposite.

Jack I don't.

Liz When we came here on honeymoon we stopped at the Metropole. Then we didn't come away for two years because Jack had hurt hissen at pit. When we came int car we came in September.

Jack Leger week. St Leger at Doncaster. Pit holidays.

Liz This is before we had our Ian or our Pamela.

Jack It's before we even thought about having our Ian, little sod.

Liz Jack, swearing.

Jack It's even before M62 is this.

Liz What a journey, can you remember it? From Upton through Wakefield to Bradford, Skipton, Clitheroe. We usually stopped at Clitheroe.

Jack Jimmy bloody Clitheroe. Allus reminded me of Jimmy Clitheroe.

Liz Our Ian used to look for the 'soap dodgers' in Bradford. Ee, it wa' funny. And there was a big hold-up at Preston. I've known us be stuck at Preston for two hours.

Jack We used to set off at six int morning.

Liz I didn't like being ont road.

Jack We set off that early one year we got to Blackpool and they were still eating their breakfasts.

Liz First time we came int car we had a bump.

Jack Ar, we did.

Liz Ee, where did we stop that year, Jack?

Jack We stopped at Beatie Fish's on St Chad's Road.

Liz We did not.

Jack We did, though.

Liz We stopped at Mavis's.

Jack Oh, ar, we did, ar.

Liz It was a lovely boarding house. Not as homely as Beatie's.

Jack We had some happy times at Mavis's.

Liz There were some funny buggers in that first year. Sam and Mary?

Jack Aye, and me and you.

Liz We were late setting off.

Jack I was ready.

Liz I wanted to go ont bus, didn't I?

Jack Ar, awkward as a broken clog.

Liz I packed that morning for some reason.

Jack We wa' listening to forecast on wireless.

Liz Not that you were listening. You were stuck in the bloody toilet, as usual.

Jack I'd just gone to t' bathroom for a shave.

Liz You were singing. I wa' on my hands and knees trying to lock the bloody case up.

Through the last sequence of lines they have transported us back in time. **Liz** *is trying to squeeze a suitcase together.* **Jack** *is standing upstage shaving.*

Liz How long are you gonna be? He's allus last minute. Don't bloody answer, Jack. I know I should've packed yesterday. Time is it? I haven't got time to get myself ready yet.

Jack I can hear you.

Liz   I wish we'd never bought that bloody car.

Jack   I can hear you.

Liz   What you doing?

Jack   I'm getting a bloody shave.

Liz   You should've got one last night.

Jack   I didn't need one.

Liz   When there's work to be done he's as scarce as rocking-horse shit.

Jack   I can hear you, Liz.

Liz   I thought you'd gone down the bloody drain. It's allus last bloody minute.

Jack (*singing*)
> The leaves of brown came tumbling down,
>   remember . . .

Liz   Jack.

Jack
> . . . in September in the rain.

Liz   Hurry up!

Jack
> The sun went out just like a dying ember.

Liz   It's every time he gets in that bathroom.

Jack
> That September in the rain.

Liz   Put a bloody sock in it.

Jack
> To every word of love I heard you whisper.

Liz   You'll make it rain if you sing like that. Shurrup!

Silence.

And hurry up. It's a quarter to seven. I thought we were getting off early in case anything happened to this bloody car. What about Preston bottleneck? I've got you a Sealeg here in case you feel badly.

Jack
My desert is waiting, dear come there with me,
I'm longing to teach you love's sweet melody.

Liz   Jack!

Jack
I'll sing a dream song for you . . .

Liz   Come on now!

Jack
Painting a picture for two . . .

Liz   If you're not down here soon I'm not going.

Jack
Blue heaven and you and I . . .

Liz   Right, that's it. I'm not bloody going. Bugger you.

Blackout.

Jack *is helping to close one of the cases.* **Liz** *is still closing hers.*

Liz   I've put yer best shirt in, in case we go anywhere special, and a couple of cardigans. And yer checked shirt and yer short-sleeved shirt. I've not put yer suit in, I've put them old trousers so that you can lounge about in 'em, and them new hankies. Is there owt else you can think of?

Jack   No.

Liz   Well, we're ready, then.

Jack   Right.

Liz   That's it, then.

Jack   We're ready then. I want to set off before there gets much traffic ont road. Come on, then.

Liz   I'll just have to check house.

Jack   What for?

Liz   I want to leave it tidy.

Jack   Why?

Liz   I want to.

Jack   There's gonna be no bugger here.

Liz   I want to leave it tidy then it's clean to come back to.

Jack   That's bloody stupid.

Liz   Have you done upstairs?

Jack   No.

Liz   Go and clean toilet. I don't want that mucky while I'm away.

Jack   This is bloody barmy, this is.

Liz   Have you switched the water off?

Jack   Yeh.

Liz   I'll leave a key next door with Mrs Witton. Then our Betty can come up on Friday and put us a fire in, warm the water up so that we can wash as soon as we get back, Saturday. Looks like there'll be some washing and all.

Jack   We haven't even set off yet.

Liz   I've got to make arrangements.

Jack   Shall I take these to t' car?

Liz   I suppose so. I do t' other.

Jack   I'll take 'em, then.

Liz I don't know why we ever had to get a car?

Jack It's a bit nippy with looks of it.

Liz I'd've sooner gone ont bus.

Jack You can go ont bus. I'll drop you off.

Liz Bloody car. It's been nowt but trouble since we got it.

Jack We've only had it a week.

Liz We could have gone ont bus, like we did ont honeymoon.

Jack You'll not get me going on t' bus again, I'll tell thee that much.

Liz Better ont bus.

Jack Aye, it bloody wa'. I smoked about twenty of other people's cigs, when we went ont bus, that much smoke about, and that was even before we'd bloody set off. There's no smoke int car, we can stop when we want, stretch your legs a bit, have a picnic. It'll not take us two minutes int car. Besides, I felt sick ont bus.

Liz I feel sick int car.

Jack I don't know how you work that out, Liz. You've only been in it once so far.

Liz I can't stand that smell. It smells of newness.

Jack What's tha want it to smell of, oldness? It is new.

Liz It's too low down for my liking.

Jack How d'you mean?

Liz It's too near the road.

Jack You'll be right. Just have another Sealeg. I'll take these.

Liz Be careful with my straw basket, it's got a flask in it. Leave it where we can get to it. It's got sandwiches in. It was a funny thing about that Popular, the newness made me feel sick, and it shook me about a lot. But I suppose it was better. Jack, tell 'em about the time we went with Chippy Baggley from Cudworth. Go on, tell 'em.

Jack No, I'm not. Chippy's this bloke who owns a local bus firm, and we'd booked one of his coaches for a trip. We're all stood, young couples, waiting for his coach to turn up. Saturday morning, half seven. At the end of this street I saw the pit paddy, that's bus we went to t' pit on. 'Look out,' I said. 'Blackpool bus's here.' Everybody looked around and laughed. Then the bus came and pulled up at the side of us. Chippy wa' drivin'. 'Blackpool?' 'Yeh.' 'Get on.' Forty of us sat sideways all the way to Blackpool with bits of coal rolling about all over the floor. That's when I started to think about gettin' a car.

Blackout.

Liz Have you put my coat in?

Jack Yeh.

Liz I've locked everything up, so we're ready.

Jack Where've you put the keys?

Liz House keys?

Jack No. Car keys.

Liz You had 'em last.

Jack You had them.

Liz I've not had 'em.

Jack You have. You went to change your cardigan in the boot.

Liz They'll be in the lock then. I left them in the lock.

Jack   No, they're not.

Liz   Oh, I put them on the top of that bag.

Jack   Which bag?

Liz   Blue one.

Jack   Where is it?

Liz   I told you to put it in the boot.

Jack   That's bloody stupid.

Liz   What is?

Jack   Fancy leaving the keys in the bloody boot.

Liz   I didn't think. I just put them down.

Jack   I've shut the boot up, haven't I?

Liz   Who're you shouting at?

Jack   I'm shouting at you.

Liz   Well, don't shout at me. It's not my fault.

Jack   Whose bloody fault is it, then?

Liz   That bloody car. Nowt but trouble.

Jack   It's nowt to do wi' t' car. It's you, woman.

Liz   If we'd packed last night . . .

Jack   Tell us another.

Liz   I wouldn't be in a rush, would I?

Jack   I don't know, and I don't care. All I'm bothered about is how to get the sodding keys out the boot.

Liz   You're gunna do it, are you? You're gunna spoil t' holiday.

Jack   *I'm* gunna spoil it. Bloody hell, Liz.

Liz   It's a great start, I must say.

Jack   Great.

Liz   In fact, that is it, this time. I'm not going. I'm not. I don't see why I should be blamed for something I haven't done. I'm not going. You spoil every-bloody-thing, shouting at this time of the morning, throwing your weight about. You'll waken Mrs Witton up with yer shouting. I'm stopping here. I'll go down to me mam's. I get blamed for bloody everything. You know what me nerves are like.

Jack   Stop here then. I'll go by my bloody self.

Blackout.

*In the blackout both **Jack** and **Liz** have sat on chairs which were arranged during **Jack***'s *story of Chippy Baggley. This is now the Ford Popular. Both are sitting in it and both are singing.*

Liz *and* **Jack**
You make me feel so young.
You make me feel like spring has sprung,
Bells to be rung,
And a wonderful song to be sung.
And when I'm feeling old and grey.
I hope I feel the way I do today.
You make me feel so young.

Liz   It's not so bad after all, int car. Is it?

Jack   No?

Liz   Wanna sweet?

Jack   Sort are they?

Liz   Barley sugars. I got them in case of travel sickness.

Jack   Yeh, I'll have one.

Liz   Do you feel sick?

Jack   No, but I'll have one. Ta.

Liz   It looks a bit cloudy.

Jack   I hope it brightens up.

Liz   We should've gone away in July.

Jack   No holidays in July.

Liz   Mind you, I've known it be nice in September.

Jack   When?

Liz   Well, me mam had a fortnight at Mablethorpe and it wa' quite good for 'um. And when she came home she looked really brown.

Jack   That'd be rust.

Liz   It only rained once.

Jack   Monday to Friday.

Liz   If you talk like that you'll but speck on the weather.

Jack   Right.

Liz   Have you got the thing?

Jack   What thing?

Liz   Boarding-house thing.

Jack   Inside coat pocket.

Liz   I wonder what it'll be like?

Jack   Woman sounded all right ont phone.

Liz   Oh, yeh?

Jack   What's it called, again?

Liz   'Beverley Guest House', Woodfield Road.

Jack   It's near football ground.

Liz   My mam said we should have gone to Beatie

Fish's. She says it's daft going to a new place, when you've been well looked after.

Jack   Sommat to do.

Liz   I hope it's clean.

Jack   You can allus give it a quick tidy up if it's not up to scratch.

Liz   I hope they haven't got any cats.

Jack   They haven't.

Liz   How d'you know?

Jack   I asked.

Liz   Oh.

Jack   Felt a right silly sod and all asking if she'd got any cats.

Liz   Look at that!

Jack   What?

Liz   That sign. There. Lancashire sign.

Jack   Bloody hell. I thought you'd seen a ghost.

Liz   Last few breaths of Yorkshire air.

Jack   Tha what?

Liz   When I wa' a kid we used to have last few breaths of Yorkshire air before we saw Lancashire sign. Fill us lungs with good air. Come on, breathe deep.

Jack *and* **Liz** *begin to take deep breaths as if they are passing the border between Yorkshire and Lancashire.*

Liz   Nearly there now, aren't we?

Jack   Are we, hell.

Liz   Wanna another barley?

Jack   Yeh.

Liz   Hey, look . . . wave at 'em.

Jack   Who?

Liz   Them Scouts are waving at us. Wave at 'em.
Hey up, are you going to Blackpool?

Jack   They can't hear you.

Liz   They're from Barnsley. Wave, Jack.

Jack *gives a curt wave to the Scouts.*

Jack   Oh, look at it, getting darker.

Liz   Are we gonna stop in a bit? I'm starvin'.

Jack   Next lay-by.

Liz   Is it spitting of rain?

Jack   It's as black as t' fire back over Chorley.

Liz   It's startin'.

Jack   Cats and dogs.

Liz   It's not forgetting to come down.

Jack   Bloody weather.

Liz   We pulled up to try and let the rain abate but it
didn't. We stopped at the spot where our Ian was sick
about ten years later. I don't know about you, but
whenever we took our Ian in the car he was always
sick at the same place, no matter how many tablets we
gave him.

Jack   I thought of writing to the Sealeg firm to claim
some money back, but I never did.

Liz   By the time we reached Preston it was still
throwing it down and we were part of the longest
traffic jam I'd ever seen.

Jack   That's Preston bottleneck.

Liz   I remember being scared because our Popular

was sandwiched behind a big van and a lorry.

Jack I was a bit worried because I was well down on petrol, and all the slow moving meant the radiator was overheating, but I never told her.

Liz No, he didn't.

Jack I kept calm. Bloody hell, come on!

Liz We wouldn't've been like this if we'd've come ont bus.

Jack Shurrup.

Liz Would we? Is there any way you can turn round? Is there another way?

Jack No.

Liz Why is it all steaming up?

Jack Where?

Liz In here.

Jack It's coz it's hot.

Liz Is that smoke coming from our car, Jack?

Jack No.

Liz Why are you whistling? Is there sommat up wi' t' car?

Jack No.

Liz He always whistled when sommat went wrong wi' t' car.

Jack Nowt's up wi' t' car.

Liz I don't like being squashed between two lorries.

Jack It's right.

Liz Aren't you a bit close?

Jack No.

Liz   Oh.

Jack   Right?

Liz   I think you are, you know.

Jack   Who's driving?

Liz   I know, Jack, but . . .

Jack   Just . . . shurrup.

Liz   Pull away, Jack.

Jack   Shurrup.

Liz   Pull away or I'm gerring out.

Jack   Liz.

Liz   Just back up and don't be stupid.

Jack   Bloody hell, woman.

Liz   Pull back.

Jack   Right.

Both actors make as if they are reversing a car. There is a sickening thump and both actors are thrown forward. There is a moment's silence.

Jack   Get out.

Liz *mimes getting out of the car, walks upstage to inspect the damage.*

Liz   The back lights and the boot were all dinted, and the lorry's lights were smashed. Ten twenty-seven W Y was all squashed up. The lorry driver jumps out of the cabin. He was furious. He gave me such a look. 'Charming.' He marched to the driver's side-window and banged on the door. 'Oi oi up, what's tha doing? Arc you bloody low, reversing in a sodding jam? Get out, I want a word with thee. Get out.' When Jack got out of the car I disappeared through the other door out of the way.

Jack *slowly gets out of the car.*

Jack 'S up?

Liz Tha' run into me.

Jack Sos.

Liz Hey up.

Jack Look, piss off. He kept saying, 'I've got your number, I'll be in touch with you.' But he never was. I had a minute, composed myself and got back in the car.

Liz *has walked back to her place in the car and is sitting quite quietly.*

Liz What did you say to him, Jack?

Jack Just said sorry and that.

Liz Oh.

Jack He could see it wa' an accident.

Liz Oh, that's all right then.

Jack I'll have another barley.

Liz We were another three-quarter of an hour in that jam. But it did mean that the rain had stopped and the sun began to come through really strongly. We used to look to see if people travelling in the opposite direction had suntans or not. If they looked pale and white then it was more likely that we would have the sun for a week.

Jack When we had our Pam and Ian we'd have competitions to see who could spot the Tower first.

Liz Jack usually won. But our Ian did well one year.

Jack It's theer, Dad, it's theer, I can see Tower.

Liz He spotted the Tower three miles outside Skipton, sixty miles from Blackpool.

Jack   It looked glorious when we arrived, all the boarding houses shone out white. The Beverley Guest House was on the sunny side of the street.

Liz   People were walking around in vests and shirt sleeves. It would be a glorious week.

Jack   We parked the car. I was glad it made it. And walked across the road.

Liz   We stopped outside, had a look through the window, and rang the bell.

Jack   There were 'No Vacancy' signs at the windows.

Liz   It must be good, Jack. 'No Vacancies.'

Jack   Ar. There were no vacancies wherever you looked.

Liz   Mavis came to the door.

Jack   A tall blonde heavy woman, with rosy cheeks and a pleasant disposition.

Liz   Hello, have you just arrived. Monroes?

Jack   Yeh.

Liz   I thought you'd never get here.

Jack   Bad jam at Preston.

Liz   I know, it's wicked in't it?

Jack   Is t' room ready?

Liz   Yes, I'll get your key. It's right at the back, turn left at the first stairs and then up two little steps. It's the one near the toilet, out of the way. Easy to find.

Jack   Easy to find? It took me half an hour to get the cases round the corner of the stairs.

Liz   Mavis kept me talking. She was a nice woman, gushy, overflowing but nice in small doses. Her husband had left her but she was making a go of the place with her partner, Gordon, a tall balding man from Lytham St Annes, who, as we later discovered, was sharing Mavis's room at nights.

Jack   Our room was tiny. I was gonna complain.

Liz   It would have been bigger had Jack been smaller.

Jack   The roof slanted down over the sink.

Liz   So he could have a wash, Jack had to bend double.

Jack   It wa' no bloody laughing matter washing the sand out of my feet when I'd been on the sands.

Liz   The room smelt a bit fusty. And the wardrobe only had one coat-hanger. Mind you, I'd brought seven of my own. I'd been caught out by that before.

Jack   Before tea we went for a walk down to the Coliseum. We saw Stanley Aklam.

Liz   They were stopping in a grubby little place down Lytham Road.

Jack   That'd suit Stanley. Whenever he went away he never took his slippers off, or his vest.

Liz   It was a smashing spread, that first tea, all the tablecloth thickly starched and the cutlery shining, the doilies were really nice and there was a fair choice of buns.

Jack   We had them little triangles of brown bread.

Liz   It was lovely.

Jack   I could've shoved them up my nostril.

Liz   We're big bread eaters.

Jack   The ham was that thin you could see through it ... I was gunna complain. I say, love, can I have a word ... ?

Liz Don't, Jack . . .

Jack Can we have another pot of tea, love, please?

Liz 'Call me Mavis,' she said. I didn't like that.

Jack You never said owt.

Liz I don't tell you everything.

Jack We had to share a table with Sam.

Liz And Mary.

Jack The noise was soft and polite.

Liz A bit like a wake.

Jack All the different tables were trying to look at each other. But trying not to be seen by anyone.

Liz Sam and Mary were different. They were fixtures in the Beverley Guest House.

Jack Smashing couple.

Liz They were in their fifties.

Jack Be long gone now, worms'll've had 'em.

Liz Sam had no teeth and said very little. Mary, it seemed, had Sam's teeth and said a lot. 'Is it your first time here? We've been here for twenty-five, is it, no, I tell a lie, twenty-two years on the trot. We came before Mavis had it. It wa' lovely then. Mavis allus saves the front bedroom for us. Oh, are you near the toilet? Well, it's handy but it's a nuisance middle o' t' night, flush flush. Are you from Yorkshire?'

Jack Ar.

Liz We're from Bolton!

Jack Used to have a good team.

Liz Mary spent most of that evening telling us her life story. Why they'd got no kids, how she met Sam.

She spared no detail. What she did for a living.

Jack What does Sam do?

Liz There was an awful silence. Mary looked at Sam. It was embarrassing.

Jack I've put my foot in it here. Only asked a simple bloody question. Bugger 'em. I had my eye on a butterfly bun. It seemed like a good time to beat Mary to it. She'd eaten most of them.

Liz He works ont sewage!

Jack Oh ar.

Liz He worked for t' council and all.

Jack Yeh.

Liz He's got some right stories to tell.

Jack I bet he bloody has.

Liz I've seen some mess in my time.

Jack Sam said.

Liz Sam came to life, telling us stories about going to the toilet, and what he'd done and seen. Jack couldn't stop laughing.

Jack Once went to this 'ouse in Bolton, Jack, terrace house, when I worked ont council, it were. They'd got a blockage somewhere. Int terrace houses manhole wa' int middle o' street. I sidles up to t' door. 'Shit van here.' 'Bit awkward, because my wife's on.' 'No trouble, I'll just nip your manhole cover off.' Well, I'm not joking Jack, when I say this, you could have eaten your dinner off that manhole. It was spotless. I couldn't understand it. Anyway, bloke came out to see what the problem was, and his son came out, and the missis next door, and we're all stood there looking down this manhole . . . Nothing . . . Spotless . . . Then slowly this water trickled past, and then this turd . . . it

was as long an thick as my arm. We all watched it
float past and then we all looked at the husband . . .
that was his wife. He blushed and looked at me and
said, 'Aye she can shit some stuff, our lass.'

Liz   We went to bed that night with Jack still
chuckling over Sam's stories.

Jack   I don't know . . .

Liz   I hardly slept a wink . . . and the toilet was flush
flush as Mary had said.

Jack   That was our first and last time in that room.

Liz   Look at this bloody room.

Jack   What's up wi' it?

Liz   It's a bugger.

Jack   You sleep int lav.

Liz   I said to ask for a big room.

Jack   I did.

Liz   I can't stop in here. It smells fusty.

Jack   Go home then.

Liz   I can't stop in here. There's no air.

Jack   Shurrup, bloody hell.

Liz   You never listen to me, do you? I said, make
sure it's a big room.

Jack   I've had to listen to you all the sodding way
here.

Liz   You never bloody talk.

Jack   We're on to that now, are we?

Liz   You've only said a dozen words all t' way here.

Jack   So?

Liz You never do owt nice . . . you're not normal. You never hold my hand or owt.

Jack It's from one thing to t' bloody next wi' yer.

Liz I wish we'd not come.

Jack I bloody do and all.

Liz You spoil every sodding thing.

Jack Do I?

Liz Yeh.

Jack I'll give yer a bloody woncer in a minute.

Liz I'm not sleeping in here.

Jack Sleep in lav then.

Liz My nerves are bloody shocking again with you.

Jack Why don't you just shurrup?

Liz Shan't shurrup.

Jack We're on bloody holiday agen, are we?

Liz Go on, shout, let every bugger hear you throwing your weight about.

Jack I shall call you sommat in a minute.

Liz Yes, you bloody start it . . .

Jack Just shut it . . .

Liz You shit.

Jack And you . . .

Liz Mavis popped up to see if everything was all right. She said, did we like the room.

Jack I said, yes, but it's small. She said she thought we'd prefer it.

Lights.

Liz The next morning was absolutely gorgeous. Jack got up early and went down for a paper.

Jack Even at half-past seven you could see that it was going to be a scorcher.

Liz We had our breakfast and got down to the sands. Just at the end of Woodfield Road are steps, which are handy.

Jack We got a couple of deckchairs from the slob who was dealing with 'em. Thanks, pal.

Liz He was nice and bronze.

Jack Don't start it.

Liz Can you put them up, Jack?

Jack Ar.

Liz He's never really been any good with his hands.

Jack I can shovel.

Liz We looked for a spot on the sands. I wanted to be near the wall in the soft sand, so we were out of the breeze. You allus get that breeze at Blackpool, no matter how sunny it is, don't you?

Jack What about here?

Liz No . . . sand's damp.

Jack Over there?

Liz No.

Jack There's space there?

Liz I wanna be int soft sand.

Jack Why?

Liz Then I can bury me feet. Look over here . . .

Jack We sat between two families of about ten each.

Liz   Five, don't exaggerate.

Jack   I like to have privacy, I don't like being near people. I can't relax, not with others about.

Liz   You can't have the sands to yourself, Jack.

Jack   Wish I could.

Liz   It irritates him. It's the same when we're at home. If there's anyone outside playing with a ball, he's up at the window seeing who it is.

There is a lighting change and both of them are sitting in their respective deckchairs. **Jack** *may be reading a book.*

Liz   Aren't you putting your trunks on, Jack?

Jack   No.

Liz   Put 'em on.

Jack   I don't want.

Liz   Get 'em put on.

Jack   No, I'm right.

Liz   Get some sun on your legs.

Jack   I'll roll my trousers up.

Liz   Tek yer shirt off.

Jack   Why?

Liz   It'll look like you're enjoying it.

Jack   I'm leaving my shirt on.

Jack   Everybody else's got their shirts off. Look! Get your stuff off, Jack, let some sun get at your body.

Jack   I'm all right.

Liz   Stanley Aklam's got his vest off. He's sat over there.

Jack   Looks like he's swallowed a coat-hanger.

Liz   They're all stripped off bar you.

Jack   They make me feel sick to look at 'em.

Liz   They're all right.

Jack   If t' cruelty man came round he'd have a field day.

Liz *produces a pair of trunks.*

Liz   Here, get these on.

Jack   I'm putting nowt on.

Liz   Nip back to t' Beverley and get 'um on.

Jack   No.

Liz   Come on, stand up. I'll hold the towel round you.

Jack   Give over.

Liz   Come on, Jack, get bloody up, get some sun on yer.

Jack   No, I'm right.

Liz   Look, get behind this towel.

Jack   No.

Liz   I can't understand you. You never enjoy yersen.

Jack   I am enjoying mysen.

Liz   You look bloody sweltered. Tek yer shoes off.

Jack   Look I'm right.

Liz   Tek 'em off.

Jack   No.

Liz   You're only bloke on Blackpool sands wi' his shoes on.

Jack   You know I don't like sand between my toes.

Liz   You allus spoil it.

Jack   I'm spoiling nowt. I'm sat here trying to sodding read.

Liz   Go on, shout.

Jack   I'm not shouting.

Liz   You could have bloody fooled me.

Jack   You can shite . . . I'm staying as I am.

Liz   Right!

Jack   Right what?

Liz   If that's what you're gonna be like all the holiday, I'm going.

Jack   Good.

Liz   I am.

Jack   Where?

Liz   I'm not sitting here with you looking like a bloody Eskimo.

Jack   Go, then.

Liz   I am . . . you spoil bloody everything.

Jack   I'm not teking my bloody shoes off so you can shit.

Liz   And you.

Liz *exits.*

Jack   Bloody woman. Do this, Jack, do that, bloody hell. I'm fed up 'on her. Tek your shoes off, she can shite. No I'm not bloody having it, I'm not. Shit to her.

Liz *enters, looking at* **Jack**.

Liz   Hello.

Jack   Are you back?

Liz   I'm going int sea.

Jack   Oh ar.

Liz   I'm going for a paddle, Jack. Are you coming?

Jack   Aye, I can do.

Liz   You're not keeping your shoes on, are you?

Jack   No, I'm gonna tek em off.

Liz   I asked a woman who was sat near to keep an eye on the stuff, while we went for a paddle. You could do that at Blackpool then, you could trust people.

The lights go out. When they come on **Jack** *and* **Liz** *are standing in the sea. They are in a bright spotlight.* **Jack** *has his shoes off and trousers rolled to the knee.*

Liz   What sea is it, Jack? North?

Jack   Irish.

Liz   Cold, int it?

Jack   'S right.

Liz   Are you enjoying it, Jack?

Jack   'S all right.

Liz   You're enjoying it, aren't you?

Jack   Yeh, it's all right.

Liz   Go on, admit it.

Jack   All right, I'm enjoying it.

Liz   I knew.

Jack   'S all right.

Liz   You're just awkward.

Jack   Ar.

Liz   We can have a walk ont pier after, buy my mam sommat.

Jack   It's bloody filthy, this water.

Liz   Is it?

Jack   Them's sewage pipes.

Liz   Wonder if Sam had owt to do with it?

Jack   Wouldn't be surprised.

Liz   Ugh . . . what's that?

Jack   Where?

Liz   I nearly stood on it.

Jack   'S only a jellyfish.

Liz   Ugh.

Jack   What's up?

Liz   Oh, look at it!

Jack   Wain't hurt yer.

Liz   Do they sting?

Jack   Ar, but it's nowt.

Liz   I'm getting out.

Jack   Why?

Liz   I don't like it.

Jack   It's bloody nowt.

Liz   Int it?

Jack   I dare eat it.

Liz   Let's go over here.

Jack   There'll be others.

Liz　We stood in that water many a time, an't we, Jack?

Jack　Ar.

Liz　When our Ian was a baby we stood with him . . .

Jack　And our Pam.

Liz　Our Ian used to lay in about six inches of water and pretend he was swimming, daft sod.

Jack　He had sand on his chest, down his trunks and all over.

Liz　They used to dig a castle wall to stop the tide coming in.

Jack　Never stopped it, though.

Liz　Our Ian used to love that.

Jack　I was a dab hand at building motorboats int sand.

Liz　Aye, he wa'.

Jack　I built one, one year, it was best I'd ever built. Then this family walked past, and they stood all over it. Some people don't care tuppence.

Liz　Our Ian wasn't bothered.

Jack　I was. It was the best motorboat Blackpool had ever seen.

Liz　I like it here, Jack.

Jack　Ar.

Liz　Just me and you.

Jack　What about these others?

Liz　Bugger 'em.

Jack　Hey up?

Liz   I don't know what to buy our Betty.

Jack   Don't buy her owt then.

Liz   Can't do that. She bought me sommat.

Jack   Oh, ar.

Liz   Look at all t' sea?

Jack   Ar.

Liz   Makes me feel as if it could sweep me up, a big wave just come and sweep me up.

Jack   Ar.

Liz   Makes me feel right small, Jack.

Jack   Thy is small.

Liz   Dun't it make you feel sommat?

Jack   Wet.

Liz   If we have kids we'll bring 'em here, paddle wi' 'em. Jump 'em over these waves. Let's jump these waves, Jack.

Jack   Gi' up.

Liz   Come on.

Jack   No.

Liz   Come on, you're enjoying it.

Jack   Oh, bloody hell.

The two of them begin to jump over waves. **Jack** *looks as if he is enjoying it. They are not holding hands, they do it on their own.* **Liz** *holds her skirt up to jump. They jump.*

Jack   This is a big 'un.

Liz   It's great.

Jack   Ohhh!

Liz   'S up?

Jack   Oh, bloody hell . . .

Liz   Jack, what's up?

Jack   My foot . . .

Liz   Eh?

Jack   I've been stung. Let me get out . . . I've been stung.

Liz   Jack?

Jack   Bleeding jellyfish!

Blackout.

Jack *goes upstage and puts on his shoes and socks.* **Liz** *remains downstage. A spotlight picks her out. She is in a queue for an ice-cream. She establishes this by looking front and back.*

Liz   Have you seen the length of this queue? That's the trouble when you want an ice-cream, you have to queue for hours to get one. Jack went back to the deckchairs sulking, trying to blame me for what happened. You can guarantee if something is going to happen to someone, it'll happen to Jack. I think I'll get a '99' cornet with a flake in it. Jack'll not want one. He can do without, for being awkward. He usually had a cornet with red sauce on it. Blood on it, he'd say. He can do without.
Some of the women, honestly, they look a right sight in bathing costumes, they're not bothered, are they? All the bodies in this queue smell of suntan lotion. Some people buy that stuff that tans whether the sun's out or not. That's bloody daft. Some of the men look quite nice. I suppose I was attracted to them really, standing close up and talking. Mind you they were a bit skinny. You could see their ribs.
'I know, int it a long queue?'

'No, only a week.'
'With my husband.'
'He's just been stung by a jellyfish.'
'No . . . I'm not . . . ?'
Some blokes'll say owt. I didn't tell Jack, he'd've
dislocated their heads for 'em.
I must have been stood there half an hour. There were
all these mothers and fathers with their kids. I started
to think, I started to think about having children. I
tried to picture Jack holding a son or daughter. I tried
to imagine him holding a dog, but I couldn't bring the
pictures into mind. I started to wonder, like you do,
whether I was capable of having children, whether I
was normal, whether Jack was normal. I had this lousy
sickening feel in the pit of my stomach that I wouldn't
be able to have children. I don't know if you've ever
gone through that stage? But . . . I was surrounded by
fathers and mothers and young men and I suddenly
felt that they were looking at me, as if they could see
that I couldn't have kids, as if it was obvious to
everyone else except me. I've never really talked about
this before . . . and I started to think . . . do I want
Jack's kids . . . do I really? What about this bloke I've
just been talking to . . . he looks nice . . . kind . . . what
about him in the ice-cream van . . . he looks like a film
star? I felt really sick, no, really sick . . . I could never
know then that our Ian would grow up to be bigger
than Jack . . . yeh, bigger than Jack . . . and successful
at what he does, or that our Pam would look like our
Betty . . . It's a funny carry on.
'What?'
'Oh, sorry, can I have a "99" cornet with a flake and
one with blood on?'

Blackout.

Liz *remains static.* **Jack** *brings her her shoes, which she puts
on. They are on the pier.*

Jack   You can say what you like, I don't like being near people. They get me down. I know that they've got to come away but when it's my holiday I'd sooner they stayed at home. You can't move for 'em. Everything becomes a bloody long drawn-out job.

Liz   That afternoon we had a walk on the Central Pier.

Jack   That's all changed and all.

Liz   I used to like looking through the wood as you walked, looking at the sands and water below. There was a bloke with a monkey who wanted to take Jack's picture.

Jack   Get lost.

Liz   Have it taken, Jack. It'll be a laugh.

Jack   I'll break t' camera.

Liz   Stand still, Jack. Let him get that monkey on you.

Jack   Is it house trained, this bloody monkey?

Liz   Smile, Jack.

Jack *freezes as* **Liz** *surveys the tableau.*

Liz   It'll look good, will that.

Jack   I bet it will.

Liz   Only one problem.

Jack   What's that?

Liz   It'll be a bit awkward working out which one's the monkey.

Jack   Shit, Liz.

Liz   Laugh, Jack.

Jack   Ha ha. That picture cost me thirty bob.

Liz It's funny, though.

Jack I can't bear people coming up to me asking me for money in the street. Like that bloke with that monkey. Pinching bloody money. Or people asking me for a poppy. I don't begrudge giving it. It's just when they come up to you in the street, it's embarrassing.

Liz Let's go in here, Jack.

Jack Where?

Liz Fortune-teller's, Madame Petrunia.

Jack Madame Shit.

Liz I bet it's good, that.

Jack Give over.

Liz She's a world-famous gypsy.

Jack Is she, bloody hell.

Liz She is. It says so.

Jack She's probably from Fleetwood or somewhere.

Liz Look, she's been with Johnny Ray. Frankie Lane. There's some pictures of her holding hands with the stars.

Jack She wouldn't be able to read my hands, nowt but calluses.

Liz I wonder what she'd say.

Jack If she told you you was going to be rich and famous, you'd believe her, wouldn't you?

Liz Yeh.

Jack And if she told you you were going to walk under a bus, you wouldn't believe her.

Liz It could be true, though.

Jack It's shite, Liz.

Liz   It's summat different.

Jack   I thought we'd come to buy yer mam sommat.

Liz   We have . . .

Jack   Well, then . . .

Liz   I know, but . . .

Jack   I'm not chucking my money away.

Liz   It's holiday, Jack.

Jack   I'm not crossing somebody's palm with silver to be told sommat I already know.

Liz   But you don't know what future'll hold for us, or are you bloody psychic?

Jack   I know this much . . . I'm gonna be working with a shovel in my hands for fifty-two bloody years, and no Madame Pinocchio'll alter that.

Liz   He was right an' all, weren't you, love?

Jack   Ar.

Liz   He's got blue marks all over his legs and back.

Jack   Liz?

Liz   That's with pit work, dust gets in your cuts . . . they go blue. First time I saw one I was nearly sick. You get used to it.

Jack   I've never been one for charms and that.

Liz   You mek your own luck.

Jack   I've not made much of my bugger.

Liz   At least the weather's held off.

Jack   Now that is luck . . .

Liz   It was stifling. I had my summer dresses on all the time. I'd brought some cardigans with me from

Marks but I didn't need them.

Jack   Everybody was sunburnt.

Liz   Except Jack.

Jack   I got my forearms brown.

Liz   An Italian-looking bloke came around the sands every day selling sunglasses. I bought a pair. Sunday, Monday and Tuesday it was beautiful. I had that Blackpool sea air on my face, I was looking well and my legs were going brown.

Jack   Wednesday morning we were back ont sands. I wa' gerrin' used to t' sun. I undid top button of my shirt.

Liz   He had his hanky on his head that he wouldn't take off, said it stopped him gerrin' sunstroke. I think he thought he was in Africa or somewhere.

They are reclined in their deckchairs. **Liz** *is wearing sunglasses.* **Jack** *has a knotted hanky on his head.* **Liz** *is applying suntan oil. This lasts for a moment.*

Jack   Burn!

Liz   Tek yer shirt off.

Jack   Shuttit. Burn.

Liz   I might tek my top off.

Jack   Leave it on.

Liz   Rub some oil on me, Jack.

Jack   Rub it yersen.

Liz   Come on.

Jack   An't you got any hands?

Liz   Sun's caught me, you know?

Jack   Has it?

Liz   I think it's clouding over. (*She administers some lotion to her arms.*) Do you want some lotion?

Jack   No, I'm natural ... Where's it gone?

Liz   Behind a cloud.

Jack   Ar.

Liz   I thought you weren't bothered about sun?

Jack   No.

Liz   It's clouding over.

Jack   Ar.

Liz   Sea's bringing it in.

Jack   Ar.

Liz   It's gonna rain.

Jack   Ar.

Liz   It's gunna chuck it down.

Jack   Bugger it.

Liz   Jack?

Jack   What?

Liz   Hold my hand.

Jack   What?

Liz   Hold me hand for a bit.

Jack   What for?

Liz   I like it.

Jack   I don't.

Liz   Please.

Jack   No.

Liz   Please!

Jack   I'm not.

Liz   Don't you like me?

Jack   Ar.

Liz   Hold me hand, then.

Jack   No.

Liz   Why?

Jack   Don't want to.

Liz   Are you embarrassed or sommat?

Jack   No.

Liz   You don't like me, do you?

Jack   Ar.

Liz   You never hold me hand.

Jack   Don't start.

Liz   I've had enough of you.

Jack   I think it's spotting of rain.

Liz   I'm fed up on it, Jack.

Jack   Ar.

Liz   I am.

Jack   It's raining.

Liz   It's finished, Jack.

Jack   Why?

Liz   You don't care.

Jack   Oh, ar.

Liz   Do you?

Jack   Get the stuff. It gunna chuck it down.

Liz   No, listen.

Jack   Look how black it is. Every bugger's going.
We're gonna get drenched.

Liz   No, I'm not going until you listen.

Jack   Look at the bloody weather. Get yer chair.

Liz   Jack?

Jack   I'm gerrin' saturated.

Liz   I am.

Jack   Come on, then.

Liz   You never take any notice of me, do you?

Jack   What do you want me to say?

Liz   I don't want you to say owt. I want you to listen.

Jack   I'm listening.

Liz   No, you're not.

Jack   Christ, Liz.

Liz   It's over, Jack . . .

Jack   Is it?

Liz   It's over.

Jack   Good.

Liz   I'm finished with you . . .

Jack   Thank God.

Liz   I'm finished, Jack, bloody lousy finished.

Jack *has left* **Liz**. *The lights have gone very dark. She is
standing on stage, rain in the background. She begins to cry. Ken
Dodd sings, 'If I Had My Way . . .' Music plays through the
interval.*

Act Two

*Ken Dodd records have been played throughout the interval. The lights dim and the music fades. **Liz** is sitting on two chairs. She has a raincoat on and her hair is soaked through. A dim blue spotlight picks her out, as does a dim light overhead.*

Liz 'When I was a young man courting the girls . . .' That's what Jack'd sing when we fell out.

'I played me a waiting game.
If a maid refused me with tossing curls,
I'd let the old earth take a couple of whirls.
Then I'd ply her with tears in place of pearls.'

Not this time, Jack.

'And as time went along she came my way
As time went along she came . . .'

'And it's a long long time from May to December,
And the years grow short when you reach
    September.'

I must have walked for miles. All the way up north . . . It was still throwing it down. I was soaked. I'd had enough, what with one thing and another. I really wasn't bothered if I never saw him again. I knew it would only get worse and it did from time to time. I looked at the sea. It was cold and grey, the tide was in, the wind had got up, and the waves were coming over on to the prom . . . I'd marvelled at that before. Now I wanted to die . . . everything was grey, nothing had any colour . . . he always takes . . . he gives nothing . . . That's what I was thinking.

Jack *enters. He too is soaking wet and is wearing a raincoat. He has obviously been walking for ages. He sits at the side of* **Liz**, *but she ignores him — he is not there. Silence for many a moment.*

Jack Hey up. Are we talking, Liz? I've been looking all over for you. Every shelter ont front. I thought you might have gone to t' Fun House. I've been in there looking for you. Look, Liz. Aren't you talking or what?

Liz Nowt to seh.

Jack You are talking, then.

Liz It's over, Jack.

Jack It shite over.

Liz And you can stop swearing.

Jack What're you doing up here?

Liz I'm sat.

Jack I know that.

Liz I wish I wa' dead, Jack.

Jack Tha dun't.

Liz I'm wet through.

Jack That's right.

Liz Am I?

Jack Look at bloody weather, eh?

Liz Ar.

Jack You wouldn't've thought it, would you? I'll lose my tan.

Liz What tan?

Jack I'm not bothered about t' rain, is tha?

Liz Have you been looking for me?

Jack Ar.

Liz All this time?

Jack I went to see if I could get some tickets.

Liz What for?

Jack A show or sommat.

Liz Oh, yeh?

Jack I thought I'd treat yer.

Liz Did you get any?

Jack I got these for t' *Student Prince* in t' Winter Gardens.

Liz I've seen *Student Prince*, Jack.

Jack I have but I know tha likes it.

Liz It's thee that bloody likes it, Jack.

Jack Tha likes it an' all, dun't tha?

Liz 'S all right.

Jack Come on, we'll get a tram back to t' Beverley, get dried off a bit.

They begin to take off their wet clothes.

It rained and rained, by the time we'd got dried off and went up to the Winter Gardens we were as damp again.

Liz When I think back, most of the dos we had were all over nothing really . . . it must have rained every September. That's where we got the song from. 'September in the Rain', Jo Stafford. Allus reminded me of Blackpool.

Jack I'd paid good money for these seats in the Winter Gardens. We were sat with all the folks who had a bob or two, you could tell.

Liz I felt underdressed. They were all posh, and dolled up.

Jack Sod 'em, I thought, my money's as good as theirs.

Liz   Only difference is that they've got more of it.

Jack   I love *The Student Prince* . . . a great show.

There is a blackout. Spotlight picks out **Liz** *and* **Jack***, sitting in the stalls at the Winter Gardens.*

Jack   This is where he goes back to her.

Liz   I know . . .

Jack   'Golden Days' is coming up . . .

Liz   I know . . .

Jack   Good set, in't it? It's good how they've done it.

Liz   Yeh . . . just watch it for a bit.

Jack   I am watching it . . .

Liz   You've not stopped telling me what's gonna happen.

Jack   Well, I want you to enjoy it.

Liz   I am.

Jack   Who's shussing me? Watch the play . . .

They watch the play for a bit and **Jack** *begins to cry. He takes out his hanky and blows his nose.*

Liz   'S up?

Jack   Eh?

Liz   What's up?

Jack   Nowt.

Liz   Are you crying?

Jack   No.

Liz   Jack.

Jack   I can't help it.

Liz   Bloody hell.

Jack It gets me . . .

Liz Bloody hell.

Jack It's good, in't it?

Liz People are looking at yer.

Jack It's nowt.

Liz Blow yer nose.

Jack I'm right now.

Liz Tha like a big kid.

Jack Nowt wrong wi' crying. I'll pee less, that's all, save my kidneys.

Liz Every time we see *Student Prince* one of us has a little cry.

Jack I did enjoy it that night.

Liz We came out of the Winter Gardens singing all the songs.

Jack 'Drink, drink, drink, to eyes that are bright as . . .'

Liz 'When it's summer time in Heidelberg there's beauty everywhere . . .'

Jack 'Golden days . . .'

Liz
'I'll walk with God from this day on,
His helping hand I'll lean upon,
This is my prayer . . .'

Jack All the way down the front.

Liz We were soaking . . .

Jack We went into Stanley's fish shop . . . had fish and chips.

Liz We had them 'sat down'.

Jack   And came out without paying.

Liz   We went to bed and slept like a log. I suppose we couldn't grumble about the weather.

Jack   No, we'd had an hour's sun.

Liz   We'd had more ... I wa' brown. It wa' sommat to show Mrs Witton when we got home.

Jack   We nearly didn't make it ...

Blackout.

Lights straight back up. They are standing at the foot of the Tower, looking up at it.

Jack   No.

Liz   Please?

Jack   No.

Liz   What about yesterday?

Jack   That's got nowt to do with it.

Liz   Come on, let's go up t' Tower.

Jack   No.

Liz   My mam's been up ...

Jack   Ar.

Liz   You're not frightened, are you?

Jack   Me?

Liz   Yeh.

Jack   No.

Liz   You are.

Jack   We've to pay to get int Tower then to pay to go up.

Liz   Once we're in though we can spend all day

looking round. We're out of t' wet.

Jack I'd sooner just walk round a bit.

Liz It's no good coming all these years . . . Didn't you go up as a kiddy?

Jack No.

Liz Not going up t' Tower, well, it's a bit like going to Bath and not seeing t' Spa.

Jack I can see t' Tower . . . it's theer.

Liz Give me some money. I'm going up it.

Jack Go.

Liz I am and you can shite . . .

Jack Don't expect me to catch thee when it falls down.

Liz Don't talk rubbish.

Jack It wa' a year ago today that somebody fell off that Tower.

Liz Tha's been reading Billy's *Weekly Liar*.

Jack It's right.

Liz A big fella like you, dare go up, bloody hell, wait till I tell our Betty and Albert.

Jack Tell 'em.

Liz You never do bloody owt.

Jack Right then . . . come on . . . and don't blame me if you're badly. I had to go through with it now. I got in the lift and there was sweat running down my legs. I didn't tell her. It wa' bloody foulest day I'd known. Stuck up theer.

Blackout.

A spotlight picks them out as they stand at the very top of the

Tower. There is a large fence around the outside of the Tower which the actors can hold. If they stand right near the audience they can perhaps better create the sense of height.

Liz   Oh, bloody hell, Jack.

Jack   Don't you like it?

Liz   I daren't move.

Jack   It's grand.

Liz   I'm scared, Jack.

Jack   I could stop up here all day.

Liz   Is it moving?

Jack   Aye, it'll be swaying a bit int breeze.

Liz   Jack, it's bloody moving.

Jack   I think that's where that bloke threw himsen into roof o' ballroom.

Liz   Jack?

Jack   Aye, it is, that must be where he fell in. They've had to put a new roof on. That's why this fence's up, stop anybody trying to throw thesen off.

Liz   Coming up's bad enough.

Jack   You wanted to come up.

Liz   Let's get down now. We've been up long enough.

Jack   'S up with yer?

Liz   I'm bloody frightened. That's what's up.

Jack   You wanted to come up.

Liz   I know I did.

Jack   You'll have to wait for t' lift.

Liz   You're off again.

Jack Ar.

Liz Can't you see that I'm shaking?

Jack Come here.

Liz You lousy fella.

Jack It's nowt.

Liz I'm not arguing over it.

Jack What're you doing, then?

Liz Shit, Jack.

Jack You shit.

Liz Don't talk to me.

Jack I wonder if I could throw you over this fence.

Liz You mck me bloody sick.

Jack I ask you. Arguing up there. If they put it in a book nobody'd believe it. I wa' wet through wi' sweat when we got down, inside and out.

Liz I wa' badly. It's nice to say that you've been up but never again in this world.

Jack I'd never known it be as bad in September. If I've ever been near dying, it was up that bloody Tower.

Liz I was glad to get down.

Jack Let's have a drink . . .

Blackout.

Liz In the Tower Lounge people were huddled together.

Jack It was packed.

Liz I had a brandy and lime. Jack had half of Sam Smith's.

Jack   Not a big drinker.

Liz   At a table near to us a group of people were smoking.

Jack *and* **Liz** *sit waiting for their drinks to come. As they wait the smoke from the opposite table begins to drift over to their table.* **Jack** *makes a cough, and* **Liz** *wipes her eyes. The smoke is bad.* **Jack** *begins to waft the smoke away with his hand.* **Liz** *helps out by using a hanky. This is insufficient. So* **Jack** *begins to blow the smoke back in the direction it came, making large blowing gestures.*

Jack   Hey up? Can you keep that smoke up there, pal?

Liz   Don't say owt, Jack.

Jack   Hey up.

Liz   Jack, don't start owt.

Jack   Who's smoking them cigs, me or you?

Liz   Jack.

Jack   I don't want that bloody filth down my lungs, pal, I've enough of that at work.

Liz   Jack.

Jack   I'm not bloody bothered.

Liz   You shouldn't say owt. They're happen on their holiday and all.

Jack   They're sat there smoking it, and then puffing it over here.

Liz   They're going now.

Jack   I'd pull his bloody arms off soon as look at him.

Liz   Settle down now.

Jack   I bloody would.

Liz Give over ... enjoy yourself.

Jack I shouldn't have said owt. I should have hit first and asked questions second.

Liz Let it bloody rest now.

Jack I ought to have given him a bloody woncer.

Liz When Jack got in 'that' mood ...

Jack Which mood?

Liz He was unbearably dangerous. It's lovely here, in't it?

Jack 'S right.

Liz You can see all t' names ont roof.

Jack Ar.

Liz They must be different composers.

Jack Yeh.

Liz I like it here ... right relaxing.

Jack 'S all right.

Liz I like it.

Jack Good.

Liz Good service, in't it? He's a nice waiter, an' all.

Jack Yeh.

Liz Pleasant.

Jack Ar.

Liz He's got a good tan, an't he?

Jack Ar.

Liz I bet he lives here.

Jack Ar.

Liz   He's a big smart fella, that waiter. Jack.

Jack   What?

Liz   That waiter's a smart-looking fella.

Silence.

He's attractive, he is. Why don't you look like that?

Jack   Like what?

Liz   Like him who's been serving us.

Jack   Do you mean that thing that's been hovering about?

Liz   He's nice.

Jack   He's shite.

Liz   Oh, he is.

Jack   When he comes back, I'm gunna kill him.

Liz   Jack?

Jack   I'm gunna kill him.

Liz   I'm only joking.

Jack   I'm not.

Liz   I only said it . . .

Jack   You said it, you bloody said it.

Liz   I wa' only having a laugh.

Jack   He's dead when he comes for these glasses.

Liz   Please, Jack.

Jack   Don't 'please, Jack' me.

Liz   Jack . . .

Jack   When I get in that mood, I'm wicked, I am, I'm evil. I'm six foot of idiot jealousy. I work in a bloody hole in the ground, and she's got the cheek to

call an article like him smart, attractive. I'd be bloody
smart and attractive if I had his job. I can't help it
when it comes over me, the mood, that is. It's like a
fog that covers me from head to toe. Nobody'll get me
out of it. She leaves me alone and I come round. I'm
not bothered about owt, only my family, everybody
else can shite. I like my privacy, I like to be on my
own sometimes. She knows what I'm like.

Liz Jack.

Jack What?

Liz I'm sorry.

Jack Ar.

Liz It rained non-stop, Thursday, so we spent a lot
of the time in a shelter on the front. We'd brought a
flask, made some coffee and had a bit of a picnic. We
did a bit of shopping and I bought our Betty a shoe
that hangs on the wall and it's a calendar. Bought my
mam some slippers from Marks . . . and Jack a white
fur cover for the steering wheel.

Jack Never bloody used it.

Liz I bought myself a shopping bag. There were
some dead cheap so I treated myself to one.

Jack Rest of the time we walked up and down,
eating fish and chips in shop doorways, mixing my
vinegar with rain water.

Liz Ugh!

Jack 'S all right.

Liz We went to Tussaud's.

Jack Ar, we did.

Liz That wa' a wash out.

Jack Wa' it heck.

Liz　I didn't think much of the Hall of Fame.

Jack　She couldn't tell who they were.

Liz　I don't think they're all that realistic.

Jack　We trailed round with a group of about fifty others all smelling and wet through in their Pacamacs like us.

Liz　Then we went into the Horror section.

Jack　Horror.

Liz　That wa' better.

Jack　I'd show 'em bloody horror. Days regular, that's bloody horrible.

Liz　If you wanted, you could go downstairs to the Anatomy section.

Jack　This was just for adults.

Liz　So we went down.

Jack　Well, bloody hell, they had specimens of bloody everything.

Liz　What's that Jack?

Jack　Dunno.

Liz　Looks like a . . .

Jack　Yeh, it does dun't it?

Liz　Oh, look at it . . .

Jack　Come on . . .

Liz　Oh, look at that . . . There was this model of a hermaphrodile.

Jack　Hermaphrodite.

Liz　I felt badly.

Jack　I felt bloody badly. Everywhere you looked

there wa' different diseases of the body. Some models showed diseases where I didn't think you could get diseases.

Liz   I wanted to get out.

Jack   And me . . . fancy paying good money to go and see bits of people's liver on show.

Liz   It wa' only wax.

Jack   I'm not bothered. I'd a sooner sat ont front in a shelter.

Liz   And we did.

Jack   I've never seen as many people walking about in the rain.

Liz   The pubs must have made a fortune.

Jack   I don't like going in at dinner times.

Liz   It dawned on me that there was nowt to do.

Jack   What about talent contest ont pier?

Liz   What about when we took our Pam?

Lights.

Jack   Now then, we've got a smashing little lady up here. Haven't we?

Liz   Yeh.

Jack   What's your name, love?

Liz   Pamela.

Jack   Pamela. And where are you from?

Liz   Don't know.

Jack   You don't know?

Liz   No.

Jack   Are you from this earth or Fuller's?

Liz   Don't know.

Jack   Don't know. Talkative, are you, Pamela?

Liz   There's my mam.

Jack   Is that your mam?

Liz   Yeh.

Jack   What are you going to do?

Liz   That's my dad.

Jack   What is it that you're going to do? Are you going to dance? Or are you going to sing? Pamela, come back to us . . .

Liz   I want to sit down.

Jack   You want to sit down?

Liz   Yes.

Jack   Aren't you going to sing for us?

Liz   Yes.

Jack   Oh, you are going to sing for us . . . that'll be good. Won't it?

Liz   Yeh.

Jack   What are you going to sing?

Liz   'My girl's a Yorkshire girl'.

Jack   'My girl's a Yorkshire girl'.

Liz   My dad sings it . . .

Jack   Your dad sings it, does he . . . in the bath . . . ?

Liz   In the house.

Jack   Oh, in the house, eh? Are you ready then? Right, off you go. 'My girl's a Yorkshire girl'.

Liz
> My girl's a Yorkshire girl,
> Yorkshire through and through.
> My girl's a Yorkshire girl . . .
> Ee by gum she's a champion . . .
> Though she's only a factory lass and wears no fancy
>   clothes
> I'm short of a Yorkshire relish for my little Yorkshire
>   rose . . .

Lights.

Jack   Well, I could have bloody eaten her, bless her.
She stood there like a matchstick and sung. There was
bloody tears running down my face . . . She didn't win
. . . but she still talks now about being in that talent
contest. She's more guts than me . . . I daren't do owt
like that.

Liz   He's a big kid is Jack when it comes to owt like
that.

Jack   It's nowt to be ashamed of, Liz. Some folks can
stand up and do stuff. Others prefer to watch.

Liz   It took me a bloody hour and half to get him
ont big dipper.

Jack   I like to stand and watch 'em now, ont big
dipper. You can see 'em get on all smiling faces and
candy floss. I like to see 'em, when they get off, being
sick, legs all wobbly.

Lights.

Liz   Are you strapped in, Jack?

Jack   Ar.

Liz   All right.

Jack   I wish I bloody wasn't strapped in.

Liz   Right, we're off.

Jack   It's slow, int it?

Liz It's slow until we get to t' top.

Jack Hey up, how bloody high does it go?

Liz To t' top.

Jack This is bloody stupid.

Liz Hold on . . .

Jack Bloody hell . . .

They are at this stage on their way down one of the slopes on the big dipper. The actors lean back in their seats and scream.

Bloody hell . . .

Liz It's great . . .

Jack I'm gonna be sick . . .

Liz Here's another one . . . whoooooooooo!

Jack Arrrrr!

Lights.

Jack I like to watch 'em . . .

Liz Going on the donkeys is about Jack's limit.

Jack That's one thing that allus gets me about Blackpool, them donkeys. They're bloody filthy.

Liz He can't stand filth.

Jack One year I took our Pam, and this donkey stunk.

Liz I wanna go on this one, Dad.

Jack Our Pam allus picked the oldest scruffiest donkey.

Liz I wanna go on Bluebell.

Jack No, go on this one . . . Dandy.

Liz No . . .

Jack   Tha don't wanna go on that one . . .

Liz   I do . . .

Jack   Pam, it stinks . . .

Liz   It dun't.

Jack   It's old, that one. Look, Dandy's young. It'll go faster.

Liz   Don't like Dandy.

Jack   It'll be a better ride . . .

Liz   Don't want a better ride.

Jack   When we got up and had a close look at Bluebell you could see the flies on it . . .

Liz   She loved going ont donkeys, our Pam.

Jack   I'm not kidding, they're pinching money up and down the country with donkey rides. Our Pam went on Bluebell. It only went about twenty yards, then it came back, it wa' ninepence a go . . . I told him . . .

Liz   Leave it.

Jack   You don't get your money's worth on here . . .

Liz   Leave it.

Jack   Well, they've only gone two bloody yards . . .

Liz   He was allus exaggerating.

Jack   I'm telling you . . . they're that bloody old Jesus must have rode on 'em.

Liz   Jack?

Jack   You snipe-nosed pig.

Liz   He was allus causing trouble, them days.

Jack   Who wa'?

Liz   You.

Jack   You've got to stand up for yourself.

Liz   He wasn't happy until things were in a turmoil.

Jack   You'd let people shit on you, you would.

Liz   You can't tell him owt.

Jack   That's what she tells every bugger we meet.

Liz   I don't.

Jack   I've told her, say nowt to no bugger. But she tells everybody her business. I tell her, you can't trust anybody, only t' family.

Liz   An' you can't trust them all t' time.

Jack   Saturday morning, it wa' lovely that year . . .

Liz   Not that year it wasn't.

Jack   It was, because I said to you, 'Look at it. We've had a lousy week and it's bloody lovely now we're going back.'

Liz   It wa' allus like that.

Jack   Not allus.

Liz   Sometimes I sit at home and when the wind's blowing and the rain's hitting the window I think of Blackpool.

Jack   I like stew meat and chips in weather like that, and bread with butter on that you can dip in your gravy.

Liz   I'll make you some of that when we get back.

Jack   Ar.

Liz   We've been thinking about changing coast for next year. Have a few days up in the north-east. Geordies.

Jack   Very friendly like us . . .

Liz   You're not bloody friendly . . .

Jack   I am when you get to know me.

Liz   Catherine Cookson lives that way on.

Jack   Grace Darling . . . her wit' lifeboats, she's from up there.

Liz   Anyway . . .

Jack   Ar.

Liz   Time is it?

Jack   Time we wa' gerrin' off.

Liz   We've a bus to catch . . . We like to sit and watch the sea. Soothing.

Jack   Ar?

Liz   Like to have a bit of a think.

Jack   It's all water under the bridge, Liz . . .

Liz   It is.

Jack   Water under the bridge . . .

Liz   I get a bit depressed when I think about my age . . .

Jack   It's one-way traffic now, Liz . . .

Liz   I hope it's not busy ont motorway. I shouldn't want owt to happen.

Jack   Bus don't go while eight. There'll be nowt ont road.

Liz   I think we'll have an hour int Tower before we go.

Jack   Can do.

Liz   I hope you have a better week.

Jack   An't it been lousy?

Liz　Typical Blackpool weather.

Jack　You've got to keep wrapped up.

Liz　It's a good job I put you them cardigans in.

Jack　Ar.

Liz　I wouldn't mind a dance . . .

Jack　No.

Liz　Are you all right?

Jack　Ar.

Liz　You look a bit flushed . . .

Jack　I'm all right.

Liz　Are you warm?

Jack　I'm rate, Liz.

Liz　You're boiling . . .

Jack　I'm bloody smothered wit' clothes . . .

Liz　Your face is red raw.

Jack　Sea air on it.

Liz　I don't know, Jack. What are we gonna make of you?

Jack　Bloody nowt.

Liz　Shall we have a walk? I don't want you drinking.

Jack　A drink'd set my blood pressure off.

Liz　I wouldn't mind a dance.

Jack　Ar . . . I wouldn't.

Lights. Music plays and they are standing centre stage waltzing together slowly.

Liz　I could never get him off the floor sometimes.

Jack   I liked a dance.

Liz   It's more of a steady walk now.

Jack   It was still raining when we came out of the Tower.

Liz   The nights were drawing in. It was dark and wet.

Jack   That sea breeze had turned a bit nippy.

Liz   I don't think we'll come here again.

Jack   Money's awkward anyhow.

Liz   Shall we get that bus?

Jack   Ar.

Liz   We walked down the prom.

Jack   In the rain.

Liz   For the last time.

Jack   When I die they can scatter my ashes on them sands.

Liz   And mine.

They pick up their cases.

All the lights were shining . . .

Jack   The Tower was lit up . . .

Liz   People were sauntering along, not bothered about the weather.

Jack   We walked past the Manchester Hotel down to the bus station.

Liz   We stopped outside the Manchester to listen to an organ playing.

Jack   Listen, Liz.

Liz   Shall we go in?

Jack   Just stand and listen.

Liz   It allus reminds me of Blackpool.

Jack   She sings it well. Come on, we'll have a last drink, bugger it!

Liz (*singing*)
   The leaves of brown came tumbling down.
   Remember, that September
   In the rain.
   The sun went out just like a dying ember.
   That September in the rain.
   To every word of love I heard you whisper
   The rain drops seemed to play a sweet refrain.
   Though spring is here to me it's still September,
   That September in the rain.

They stand singing in the rain. Rain sound is heard and above their singing is the singing of Jo Stafford. As the lights fade **Jack** *exits, brings a half of beer and a brandy and lime for* **Liz** *to drink, they sit, toast each other, then they toast the audience. The actors bow and leave their cases on the stage. Ken Dodd sings 'Tears for Souvenirs'.*

Salt of the Earth

Salt of the Earth was commissioned by Wakefield 100 and first presented as part of the Wakefield Centenary celebrations at the Theatre Royal and Opera House, Wakefield, in 1988. It was subsequently rewritten and presented by the Hull Truck Theatre Company at the 1988 Edinburgh Festival, where it won a Fringe First Award, and then as part of the Perrier Pick of the Fringe Season at the Donmar Warehouse, London, with the following cast:

May	Maggie Lane
Annie	Amanda Orton
Roy	Nigel Betts
Harry	William Ilkley
Paul	Nigel Betts
Kay	Julie Gibbs
Tosh	Adrian Hood
Mr Poole	Adrian Hood
Mrs Potter	Julie Gibbs
Mrs Gillespie	Julie Gibbs
Cherry	Julie Gibbs

Directed by John Godber
Designed by Robert Jones

Act One

West Yorkshire. 1947.

The stage is pre-lit. Music: Judy Garland's recording of 'The Trolley Song' plays. The house lights go down and the lights change to deep blue to give a night effect.

Annie Parker, *aged sixteen, dressed as a work girl in overalls and a headscarf, rushes on carrying a coat and a bag. She is late, and puts on her coat while calling to her sister off stage.*

Annie May . . . May . . . What's she doing now? May? Come on . . . She's allus fiddling about. Come on . . . what are you doing?

May Parker *enters, even more untogether than* **Annie**. *She is eighteen.*

May I'm coming, aren't I, let me get me things.

Annie It's fish and chip night, Fridays.

May I know.

Annie Me dad'll never been able to keep 'em warm ont' oven top.

May I hate fish and chips. I put mine in the dustbin.

Annie What have you been doing?

May Cleaning all your mess up.

Annie I didn't leave any mess.

May You did.

Annie I did not.

May You did, Annie, you left oil dripping all over the place. You've got to leave your work-tops clean, you know that. As soon as the hooter went you were off like a whippet.

Annie I don't want to miss the bus, do I?

May There's plenty of time.

Annie Not if it's full.

May We can get the next one.

Annie But I won't have time to get a bath.

May You will.

Annie But I want to soak.

May Annie, you always get carried away.

Annie I can't wait to see Roy, can you?

May What do you want to see Roy for?

Annie Well. Don't you want to see Harry?

May Not really; all we do is argue. I don't know if I even like him.

Annie I don't know what to wear.

May I haven't got much choice.

Annie I think I'll put that yellow frock on.

May Does Roy like that?

Annie I think so.

May Ask him. They're working under here. There's coal-faces all under here. (*Shouting to the miners.*) Roy? Harry? Can you hear us. Are you there? Is anybody there?

Annie (*seriously*) Roy?

May She's putting that yellow frock on again, Roy. Knock twice if that's OK.

Annie Do you think they can hear us? Roy ... It's me agen ... I love you ... we're going to have lots of children ... I'll see you in the ballroom at half-seven.

We're having fish and chips for tea, our May doesn't want hers. You won't be able to come home tonight because me dad's staying in. This is Annie Parker saying: I'll see you at the Welfare.

May I wonder about you, Annie.

Annie Oh look . . .

May What?

Annie Come on . . .

They both exit at speed.

The lights change. Music: Bing Crosby singing 'Piociana'.

Two miners, **Harry** *and* **Roy**, *crawl to the music across the stage.* **Harry** *is downstage,* **Roy** *is upstage. They have shovels and they begin shovelling together.*

Harry These are our pits now tha knows, Roy. We own these buggers.

Roy Doesn't make the shovelling any bloody easier though, Harry, does it?

Harry They're our pits now, old cock, people'll always need coal, job for life, this bugger. They need us, old lad.

Roy They can have the bloody job for my money, I'm sick on it.

Harry It's a man's job, what's up wi' thee?

Roy Is it warm or am I having a bloody stroke?

Harry It's warm, we'll fill this off and then go up to three's junction. It's cooler.

Roy About time, I'm just about ready to drop my pants.

Harry Bloody hell, well do it down wind of me will you, my stomach's a bit dodgy as it is.

Harry *continues with his shovelling. He begins to sing 'If You Were the Only Boy in the World'.* **Roy** *watches him and crawls to him.*

Roy Oi oi oi . . . can tha whistle?

Harry Why?

Roy Because tha can't bloody sing.

Harry Tha named the day yet?

Roy Not yet, have you?

Harry Thinking about it. Hey, have you seen their father?

Roy No.

Harry He works in the headings; they reckon he can pick up an iron-girder by hisself.

Roy Give over, I can feel thee pittling down my back.

Harry It's rate. Two men can't lift an iron-girder. Don't bloody cross him; when he says put the locker in the back wheel, put it in the back wheel.

Roy I'm getting out, tha knows, I'm not having this.

Harry What's up wi' you? It's smashing.

Roy It breaks my heart to come down here when the sun's shining.

Harry Well, when tha gets up in a morning, shut thee eyes.

Roy I'm not having this all my life.

Harry Don't you like it?

Roy Oh ay . . . I likc it. But there's too much fresh air for me.

Harry Has tha heard about the new under-manager?

Roy What about him?

Harry He's nine foot seven, only a young lad.

Roy Oh ay . . . and has he got two heads?

Harry They reckon he's a right swine . . .

Mr Poole, *the under-manager, crawls to where they are working.*

Roy Tha going to t' Welfare 'Free 'n' easy' toneet?

Harry Be a wonder if I don't. I haven't missed a dance in the last two years.

Roy I think they've got a new band on.

Harry They have.

Mr Poole What the bloody hell are you two doin'?

Harry We're getting this off the face as fast as we can before he shits his pants.

Mr Poole I thought you'd stopped.

Roy Are you the man they've sent from the market pool.

Harry Here grab a shovel, we need a hand, it's bloody horse-work is this. Come on here.

Roy Start down that end if you want, we'll work to meet you.

Mr Poole Do you know who I am?

Roy No.

Harry What's he say?

Roy He says, do we know who he is?

Harry I don't know who he is.

Roy Bloody hell.

Harry Poor bloke.

Roy Fancy not knowing who you are. Hey sorry, mate, I can't help you, we don't know who you are.

Mr Poole I'm the new under-manager, I'm Mr Poole.

Harry Oh bloody hell, we've done it now, Roy.

Roy Sorry, Mr Poole. For a moment there I genuinely thought you didn't know who you were.

A moment. Music: 'String of Pearls'. The lights change.

Everyone exits. **Annie** *and* **May** *come on dancing.*

A mirror-ball spins. We are at the Miners' Welfare.

May Every weekend we would dance to a new band at the Miners' Welfare.

Annie We'd put into practice the dance steps we had learnt at home.

They dance together, and fill the stage.

May You remember what happened the first time Harry called at our house?

Annie Even if I can remember, you'll still tell me.

May Me dad was in the bath, he'd just come in from afters. Harry was waiting outside the front door. When he knocked on the door me dad opened the bathroom window, saw who it was, and threw a bucket a' mucky bath water all over him.

Annie Why?

May He hated Harry, because he came from Upton.

Annie Well, it is three miles away.

May I'd known him a year even then.

Annie What, before you brought him home?

May Yeh.

Annie Bloody hell.

May We didn't do a lot that night.

Annie No?

May No, we stayed in and sat by the fire until he dried off. He's got a weak chest, you know? Nearly caught his death.

Annie Me dad's a bugger.

May We'd been courting about eighteen month, and I think somebody must have told him at t'pit that I was seeing Harry, and that we were going to the pictures. So ... anyway we come out of the pictures and who's there waiting for me?

Annie Me dad ...

May I could have bloody died.

Annie They get on now though, don't they?

May Oh yeh.

Annie Thought so.

May But they don't talk.

Annie That's probably why they get on.

May If me dad strung a sentence together he'd bloody choke hissen.

Annie I think he likes Roy.

May Yeh, I think he does.

Annie (*to the audience*) During the early fifties the four of us went everywhere together.

May We were one big family.

The lights change. The mirror-ball is struck.

Roy *and* **Harry** *enter with picnic gear, they are dressed in suits in the height of fashion.*

Roy   Every weekend we got on a bus and got away from it all.

Annie   Harry would try his hand at singing.

Harry *sings a few lines of 'Hold Me, Hold Me'.*

May   And Roy would tell awful jokes . . .

Roy   Right, there's these two nuns.

Harry
May } *(together)*   We've heard it.

Annie   And we went dancing to the Palais de Dance at Hemsworth, Tassels at Royston.

May   The Astoria at Goldthorpe

Annie   We went on mystery trips.

Roy   Where the bloody hell are we?

Annie   Club trips to Cleethorpes. Racing at Doncaster. We had picnics in Pontefract Castle, and these two went swimming in Ponte Park . . . it seemed to me that every day was a holiday.

They sit together. Silence.

Roy   I don't think we're going to have any kids for a few years.

Harry   Why, don't you know what to do?

Roy   Why, what do you do?

May   If you don't know, Roy, I'm not tellin' you.

Annie   I'll tell you after, love.

Roy   Yeh . . . I'm a bit slow when it comes to things like that. Don't the storks still bring 'em?

Annie   Roy says we should wait a bit.

Roy   I'm gunna get out of the pit, Harry. Get involved in a sat-down job, make a fortune, and come back and live in a big house. And then you two . . .

May When we're old and wizen'd . . .

Roy You two'll say 'they bloody did it'.

Annie We'll have a big house.

Roy Oh ay, we'll have a big house, we'll be known as the folks who live on the hill . . .

Annie And then after the first million, then we'll have kids.

Harry Bloody hell, you'll be rusty by then.

May I think I want a son.

Roy Oh bloody hell, look out, Harry.

Harry You don't want it now, do you?

May Why?

Harry I've got a headache . . .

Annie Oh you silly sod . . .

Laughter.

A bloody headache?

May No, I want a son, an' he'll be a big strapping lad, like me dad.

Harry And he'll work with me down t'pit . . . So as I shall seh, nip up there, kid, and bring me some sandwiches, be a good lad.

May He'll not go down t'pit. He'll work in a bank.

Harry He could work in Roy's business.

Annie That's a good idea, we could make it a family affair, like McAlpine's. I'll be Roy's secretary, Harry can be one of the workmen.

Harry A scrubber?

Annie   Yeh a scrubber, Harry, yeh ... And our May can make the tea ...

May   Bloody typical that is and all.

Roy   Roy and Annie married in nineteen fifty-four, true to Roy's cavalier fashion they honeymooned in France. They had four days in Paris.

Annie   Me dad was ill for three days when I got married. He cried all through the ceremony and all through the reception.

Roy   They bought a house in Kirkby, after all, it was an investment.

Annie   Roy was very handy about the house, he would put up shelves, decorate and keep the garden tidy. He built a rockery, and painted two little gnomes and even made a bird-bath.

Roy   I might build a fishpond.

Annie   A fishpond? What for?

Roy   To put bloody fish in.

Annie   Don't be daft, we don't want a fish. Nobody in Kirkby has a fishpond.

Roy   We will. It'll put value on the house.

Annie   But next-door's cat might eat the fish.

Roy *and* **Annie** *exit with the picnic gear.*

May   May and Harry were married in nineteen fifty-five. They had waited till after Christmas so they were in a new tax year, and with the tax they both got back, Harry bought a new car ... I wanted to buy a house ...

Harry   Ha ha ha, a new car ... best car down Clayton Street.

May   So we moved into a rented pithouse. The move

to Upton upset me dad; he seemed to be morose all
the time, now me and our Annie had left home. He
was completely alone.

Harry He'll manage, he can visit when he likes.

May I felt a great sense of freedom, living in my
own house.

Harry We had a new car at the garden gate.

May And an enormous gramophone-cum-wireless.

Harry It was all we needed.

Time has passed. Music: 'Begin the Beguine'.

May *and* **Harry** *dance.* **Roy** *and* **Annie** *come on, carrying
chairs.* **Annie** *is very elated.*

Annie Oh my God ... Oh my God ... I don't
believe it.

May Settle down ...

Annie *screams.*

May Annie? You're delirious.

Annie What'll me dad say? I'm going to be an
aunty. Bloody hell, Roy, I'm going to be an aunty,
what do you reckon?

Roy I didn't know you had it in you.

May I can't believe it ... I just can't.

Harry I know I look a bit slow, Roy, but I know
how many beans mek five.

Annie When's it due?

May It?

Annie Well ... you know what I mean.

May February.

Roy   Well, I suppose congratulations are in bloody order. Well done, May love ... smashing, I'm proud of you.

Roy *leans and kisses* **May**.

May   Thanks, Roy.

Roy   Well done, you bugger ...

Harry   She's the bloody hero, Roy, she's got to go through all the agony.

Annie   You're so cheerful.

Roy   Uncle Roy! Bloody hell, I feel like I've just been knighted ... Hey, we want to take him out you know, when he's here.

Annie   He? Might be a she.

Roy   Might be.

Harry   What about you two?

Roy   We're waiting to see what happens. If this newsagent's shop in Wetherby comes off, we'll be up and off.

Harry   You want to be careful, you know, Roy. I knew a bloke who once bought a paper shop ...

Roy   Ay, and it blew away, I know it.

May   We've got a lot of things to do in the house before I have it. And he's next to bloody hopeless with his hands. When we first got married he couldn't make a cuppa tea.

Harry   I can boil an egg.

May   He's the only fella I know who actually burns water.

Harry   Any chance she gets to have a dig at me, Roy, she will do.

May I'll tell you what he does.

Harry Oh spare us.

May No . . . I want our Annie to hear this. He comes home from the pit, and he's that bloody tired, and such an idle sod, he goes to sleep on the kitchen floor in his pit-muck.

Harry Once, I've done that, once.

May More than bloody once.

Annie You don't want to be letting her do all the fetching and carrying now, Harry.

Harry I don't do, Annie.

May He bloody will.

Harry I won't.

May I have to do the bloody garden.

Annie Can't Harry do it?

Harry I get hay-fever.

Annie Make sure she's all right, you know?

Harry I will.

Roy Course he will, bloody hell, you always look on the black side.

Harry I'm going to make sure everything's perfect for her, aren't I?

May I want some bloody new lino going down in that back passage.

Harry I'll see to it, leave it to me. I'm not kidding, Annie, your May is house mad.

Annie You shouldn't let her overdo it.

Harry I won't.

May   He's not a bad old foul pig of a fella.

Roy   She loves him to bloody death.

May   He's a worm, Roy, but I love him . . .

Music: 'Elmer's Tune'. **Harry** *walks to a spotlight downstage centre.*

May *exits.* **Roy** *and* **Annie** *remain frozen.*

Harry (*to the audience*)   In nineteen fifty-six May gave birth to a big baby boy. He was born at Southmoor Hospital, Hemsworth, and weighed ten pounds at birth. May was severely ill, she was in a coma for twenty-four hours, had a blood transfusion, and didn't see her son till a full four days later. When she did see the baby, her eyes lit up, and she smiled a smile so wide that I thought her face would split in two. She was so proud, so full of happiness and warmth and for the first time in our lives, I think we understood the meaning of the word 'love'.

Blackout.

Harry *exits.*

Roy *and* **Annie** *come to life. The lights come up.*

Roy   I never looked at Betty Lewis.

Annie   I saw you looking at her at the dance.

Roy   I never was!

Annie   You were I saw you, every time she passed our table you couldn't stop yourself from having a look at her.

Roy   All right, all right, I was looking at her, can't I bloody look at another woman now, can't I even speak to another woman?

Annie   It was the way you were looking.

Roy   What am I supposed to do if I go into a bloody

shop and a nice woman comes to serve me? What am I supposed to do, ask for a bloke to serve me. For God's sake grow up, or get bloody lost.

Annie I can't help being me, Roy.

Roy I know that . . . bloody hell, I know that much.

Annie Do you think I want to be like this? Do you think I want to be upset all the time? Do you think I don't want to have kids?

Roy Leave it now, let's not start all that again.

Annie How do you think I feel inside?

Roy I know how you feel, Annie, I feel the same myself. Forget it now.

Annie I can't just forget it.

Roy It's not your fault, is it? Nobody's blaming you. Don't take it out on yourself.

Annie Our May was the one who was always ill as a kid, and she's OK . . . I can't understand it.

Roy Leave it now . . .

Annie But I want kids, Roy, I want 'em.

Roy I know you do. I was the one who said we'd wait.

Annie I feel so empty inside. I feel like my whole inside is rotting away. I wish I could rip my stomach out.

Roy Stop getting worked up, Annie, stop it! We've been over this a million times; we've seen every bloody specialist in the area. There's no chance, listen to me, no chance. So that's it. It's over, forget it. Let us please just get on with our lives . . .

Annie Don't tell our May.

Roy   Why am I going to tell your May? What am I going to do, run round and tell her?

Annie   I don't want anybody to know.

Roy   Nobody will. Now bloody calm down. It's not the end of the world. We've got each other, bloody hell, we've got each other.

Annie   I wish I could start my life all over again, Roy. I wish I could wipe the slate clean. Start afresh.

Roy   When we get this paper shop in Wetherby it'll be a whole new life for us.

Annie   I feel like I've let you down.

Roy   Don't be daft.

Annie   I love you, Roy ... I don't think I could live without you.

The lights fade to deep blue. Music: Dick Haymes 'You'll Never Know'.

Roy *and* **Annie** *dance off.* **May** *enters. She wears a headscarf and is pushing a pram. She stands in a spotlight.*

May   Me dad was over the moon when he saw the baby, he didn't say much to Harry, just told him to look after me, and then he started to cry. We took him down to me dad's regular. Me dad would just stand with the pram looking at him, never saying a word. Then one day I overheard him saying 'I'm thee grandad'. On Sunday afternoons our Annie would take him up on to the common.

The lights change. It is 1957.

Annie *enters and takes the pram from* **May** *who exits.* **Mrs Gillespie** *enters.* **Annie** *pushes the pram downstage right,* **Mrs Gillespie** *follows her.*

Mrs Gillespie   Oh he's smashing, int he?

Annie Yeh.

Mrs Gillespie He's lovely, aren't you? How old is he?

Annie Thirteen months.

Mrs Gillespie Oh he's smashing.

Annie Yeh, it's a bit cold to have him out though.

Mrs Gillespie It'll blow the cobwebs off him. Yeh?

Annie Yeh.

Mrs Gillespie You'll be glad to have got him out of the way. That's what I thought when I had my first. Get the first one out of the way and then you're laughing. I mean look at me daughter. Twenty last week and she's had a little girl, oh she's smashing and all, cheeky little face she's got. I wanted to call her Kathleen, but they've christened her Kay ... Oh look at him, he's smashing. She's got the first one out of the way ...

Annie First? Yeh.

Mrs Gillespie You take my word for it, love. The first is always the worst. Oh, but he is lovely, he is. Look here's sixpence for him.

Annie Oh thanks.

Mrs Gillespie How's your dad?

Annie You know, getting by.

Mrs Gillespie Your May married yet?

Annie Yeh, married, lives in Upton.

Mrs Gillespie Oh ... Has she had any?

Annie No ... no not yet ...

Mrs Gillespie Well, there's time for her, int there?

Annie Yeh.

Mrs Gillespie But he's smashing he is, aren't you?

Annie The nurse said I'd got to bring him back when he was twenty-one.

Mrs Gillespie I should think so and all. He's bloody smashing.

Mrs Gillespie *leaves.* **Roy** *appears.* **Roy** *and* **Annie** *look into the pram.*

Annie Don't wake him, Roy.

Roy I'm not doing . . .

Annie You are . . .

Roy I'm not . . . (*Singing.*) 'Hush-a-bye baby on the tree top, when the wind blows the cradle will rock . . .'

Annie What did they say?

Roy Three weeks.

Annie (*shouting*) Three.

Roy Sssshh. Three weeks, and we can move into the shop. We can get away from Kirkby, I can get out of that shit-hole and we'll be living it up in Wetherby . . .

Annie And he'll be able to come and see us, won't you, eh? You'll have to come and visit your Aunty Annie and Uncle Roy, in their big new house in Wetherby . . .

Roy You'll like that, won't you? Eh? We'll have a swing, and your Uncle Roy'll make a tree-house.

Annie I want to adopt, Roy.

Roy I know.

Annie I do.

Roy I know you do.

Annie   Promise we can.

Roy   Yes.

Annie   Promise.

Roy   Promise. Cross my heart hope to die.

Annie   I can't believe that it's all happening like we planned.

Roy   Well it is . . .

Annie   Well, kiss me then.

Roy   I'll kiss you after.

Annie   Kiss me now.

He does so.

See that, Paul, did you see that? Your uncle Roy kissed me then. Mmmmmm. (*To the baby.*) Mmmmmmm. Shall we go to the dance tonight?

Roy   If you want to go to the dance, we'll go to the dance.

Annie   Shall we take you back to your mam, shall we?

The lights change. Music: Bing Crosby's 'Piociana'. **Roy** *and* **Annie** *leave the pram and go upstage left and dance in a spotlight. A wind machine howls.*

May *enters and stands centre in a spotlight.* **Harry** *enters in mining gear and moves into a spotlight downstage right.*

Harry   We were working in the new face, three's face, very low, very warm, no room to move, like being in a bath of dust, more room in a tub, couldn't turn around, blackness and noise all about, and the beams of light sent shadows all over your world. Your world was two feet nine high, black, grit black, shiny black coal. Me and Roy are working; it's snap time, I tell him that I'm going up to three's junction snap there, it's cooler, more room. And we're snapping, and I have to drop me pants, there's no shit-house down there, and Roy says 'Go as far away as you can, I've got luncheon meat on my bread.' So I did. I walk for five minutes up through three's heading just to drop me pants. And Roy was sat there chuntering to hissen, sat alone, eating luncheon meat. (*Quick pause.*) And the roof went, a junction girder collapsed, letting the junction in; a large steel, strong . . . girder collapsed. Two hundred tons of stone came crashing in.

Mr Poole (*off*)   There's an accident in three's junction.

Harry   Two hundred tons of stone came crashing down pinning him to the floor, nailing him to the dust. The noise was deafening. *Roy!*

Annie   Roy!

Roy *stops dancing and exits.*

May   Roy!

Harry   *Roy.*

Mr Poole (*off*)   Get some men down there.

Harry   Dust, like fog, dust so thick it clogged up your every pore, settled in your lungs like sand in an hour-glass. Roy! We managed to get him out, twelve men dug him out. A doctor administered morphia. He was alive when they brought him out of the pit. I told Annie, 'Don't worry, love, he's alive, he was alive when they brought him out of the pit.' He was alive when they brought him out of the pit – that's what they said . . . But how could he be? He was crushed to death, crushed to a wafer. He died on the way to hospital. I felt so sorry for Roy, but I felt even more sense of sorrow for those he's left behind.

A howling wind is heard. **Harry** *slowly turns and leads* **May** *and his son in the pram off.*

Annie *stands alone centre, lit by one spotlight. The wind blows. She is in utter grief.*

Annie   Oh God ... oh God ... Oh my God ... HELP ME ... HELP ME ... Roy ... Oh God ... Roy ... Roy ... I wish the earth would burn up. I wish every piece of coal in the earth would burn up ... every rotting coffin catch light. I wish every miner was dead ... I do, that's what I wish ... I wish every miner was dead ... Roy, Roy, ROY, ROY!

Music: Bob Hope's 'Thanks for the Memory' and fades slowly. Meanwhile, the lights change.

Mrs Potter, **May**'s *neighbour, is frozen in a spotlight upstage.* **Annie** *exits.*

When the music has gone, **Mrs Potter**, *with a lighted cigarette, steams downstage to call her son in. The lights change.*

Mrs Potter   Ian ... Ian? Get in this bleeding house now.

May *enters with a brush, sweeping up the soil which has been thrown by the neighbours.*

May   Look at the soddin' mess.

Mrs Potter   Come on here, I shalln't say it agen.

May   I'm not having it, you know, love.

Mrs Potter   Not having what?

May   All this soil on my path.

Mrs Potter   There's only two pieces!

May   I'm not bothered. I've had to sweep it up twice already.

Mrs Potter   Get in this bleeding house now!

May   You can't control your kids.

Mrs Potter   Come on here.

May That young 'un of yours is going to catch its death. He's running about with no shoes and socks on, bare-arsed.

Mrs Potter That's my bloody business.

May I don't want 'em throwing soil on my path, not when I'm trying to keep my house tidy ... And you could do with some soap and water round your house, instead of going to the club every bloody dinnertime ...

Mrs Potter Don't waste your bloody breath. If you want to kill yoursen cleaning up all the bloody time, bully for you ...

May You little worm, I'll break your bloody nose ...

Mrs Potter Oh pull the other one, Mrs Hickman, it's got pissing bells on ... Come on here ... now!

Mrs Potter *exits.* **Harry**, *tired and moody, returns home. The lights change.*

May Late.

Harry Am I?

May Wondered where you were?

Harry Cemetery.

May Tea's ready.

Harry Don't want any.

May Don't have it then.

Harry I just called to see him, first time since, nice headstone. Don't reckon much to the verse.

May Our Annic picked it.

Harry Typical.

May Tea's on. Be stewed by now. All settlemented.

Harry I heard you the first time.

May Only saying.

Harry Only saying? You're getting on my bloody nerves with it.

May You're getting on mine.

Harry Am I?

May They're a bloody nuisance them next door. She can't control them kids. If our Paul turns out like them I'll kill him.

Harry Where is he?

May Int room . . . Now get your tea.

Harry Where's the butter on this bread?

May Why?

Harry Where's the butter?

May On the bread.

Harry I don't call that butter, I like a lot of butter, not just a wipe.

May Get it eaten.

Harry Call that butter?

May What do you call it, shit?

Harry I want a lot of butter when you butter my bread.

May Do it your bloody self next time. You never do anything in this bloody house. You're useless.

Harry You're the woman . . . I bring the money in. You do everything in this house. Or do you want to swap jobs, and go down that shit-hole every day.

May You never do a bloody thing, you don't.

Harry   You silly woman.

May   Stop shouting.

Harry   I'll swing for you. This is my house, I pay the rent here and I want more butter on my bread, do you hear me?

May   You'll get it on, you'll get it . . . I'll put that much on next time, it'll bloody choke you to death.

Harry   Go on shout, you daft sod, that's all you bloody do.

May   You're the one who's shouting, not me. You're the one who brings unpleasantness into this house, you, not me.

Harry   You must be joking, every time I come home you've got a face as long as a wet week. I can't help it if you can't get on with the neighbours. You're like your father, unsociable, you can't talk to people.

May   Why don't you shut your silly bloody mouth? Go to bed, you're that tired you don't know what you're saying.

The lights change. Music: Nat King Cole 'When I Fall in Love'. **May** *and* **Harry** *freeze.*

Annie *enters. She looks older and drawn.*

Annie (*to the audience*)   There were no arguments in my house, everything was still and quiet. And even in nineteen sixty-five, despite Elvis 'n' Gene Pitney, I still cried for Roy. I had tried to meet another man at the Welfare Dance, but I'm not that sort of person. I was coping by myself. Just.

Harry   But in nineteen sixty-six tragedy struck the Parker sisters. Big John Parker their father died of a heart attack.

Annie   He was buried next to me mam, and was, we

all hoped, the last Parker to lose his life for coal.

May   Me dad had had pneumoconiosis for years, but the doctor insisted that that wasn't the cause of death.

Harry   May was shattered when her father died, she became even more neurotic, and the smile that she often smiled in her youth was seldom ever seen.

Annie   During this time Harry had a number of minor accidents at the pit. He'd lost two toes off his left foot.

Harry   And I had the top of my thumb taken off, but it was nothing to get excited about, and I could still dance.

May   If anything he was all the more nibbler.

Annie   May poured all her interests into Paul – he couldn't trump in public without his mother knew about it.

The lights change. **Annie** *and* **Harry** *exit.*

May *turns to the audience.*

May (*shouting*)   Paul? Paul?

Paul *answers, off, then enters. He is ten years of age, with big ears. He wears short pants.* **Tosh**, *the same age, is also in tow.*

Paul   Paul Hickman was an only child and in nineteen sixty-six he was a ten-year-old marble champion. Having just beaten his best friend Tosh for six large bollies. He was the best marble player in Upton.

May   Come on, it's half-six.

Paul   Can't I stay out? Tosh is.

Tosh   Me mam lets me stay out till eight.

May   No, come on, your dad'll be home soon.

Paul Oh Mam, we've got another championship to play.

May Well you'll have to play it tomorra, I want you in the bath.

Paul Why do I allus have to come in early?

May 'Cos you do, I've got my routine. Tosh can stay out because his mam washes the little 'uns first.

Paul But, Mam?

May I want you in, now. The more sleep you have the more intelligent you'll be when you grow up. Now come on, I've got some boiled fish for your supper. Fish for brains my mam used t'say.

Tosh See you tomorra. Play a twenty-niner...

May Paul, come on, now!

May *exits.*

Kay Cooper, *aged ten, suddenly arrives on stage.* **Paul** *and* **Tosh** *look at her.*

Kay Are you playing marbles?

Tosh No, he's got to go in.

Kay Why?

Tosh His mam ses.

Kay I can stop out. Me mam ses I can stay out till nine o'clock.

Tosh Nine o'clock?

Kay Yeh. Are you playing then? I've got some bollies.

Tosh Play a twenty-niner?

Kay Yeh ... me name's Kay ... come on ...

Tosh Are you coming?

Paul Can't. Me mam'll hit me.

Tosh I'll see you.

Paul She's a lass . . .

Tosh I know. See you.

Paul Zig.

Tosh Zog . . .

Tosh *leaves with* **Kay**. **Paul** *watches them go.*

Music: 'Begin the Beguine'.

Paul (*to the audience*) I don't think I'll ever forget those years . . . I failed my eleven-plus, and I didn't get a racing bike: I got a good hiding instead. I think me mam 'n' dad were embarrassed because I'd failed. Most other kids in our class had passed. But I wasn't really bothered. What I resented most though in nineteen sixty-seven was having to go to bed when it was still light outside, I would lay awake and listen to Tosh and the other kids playing French cricket or Best-Man-Falls . . . and downstairs I could hear me mam 'n' dad dancing to old-time records . . .

Music: a slow foxtrot.

Harry *and* **May** *enter dancing.*

May We were the best dancers at the Welfare.

Harry Slow, slow, quick quick, slow.

Paul (*to the audience*) Me mam said that going to bed early would make me intelligent, but I had my doubts about that. During this time me dad used to pinch my nose and pretend that he had it in his hand, and he was forever showing me a trick where his thumb seemed to split into two pieces . . . I was beginning to think that it was me dad who should go to bed early.

Paul *exits.*

May *and* **Harry** *still dance, then they drift apart.*

Harry   Comc on . . .

May   No . . .

Harry   Yes.

May   I can't cope with another one, not at my age.

Harry   All you had to do was have him, I washed all the nappies, I did all the shitty work.

May   I'm not arguing about it, I'm not having another kid and that's that . . .

Harry   I bloody hate you sometimes.

May   Ay and I hate you.

Harry   Well tek off then, sling your hook.

May   Shurrup shouting this time of night.

Harry   I shall shout if I want, it's my house.

May   Go on then, shout, you're like a big soft kid, shouting because he can't have his own way. Banging bloody doors and shouting . . .

Paul *enters dressed in his pyjamas.*

Paul   What's up, Mam?

May   Nowt, go back to bed.

Harry   Paul, tell your mother that she's a foul pig of a woman.

May   And tell your dad he can shit.

Harry   Tell her that I'm going to Sheffield and I'm not coming back.

May   Tell him: good.

Harry   Tell her, I mean it.

May   Tell he, he can do what the bloody hell he

likes. In fact, you can tell him that I'll leave, I'll go down to our Annie's, she's fed up of being by herself. He can have all the bloody housework, see how he likes it.

Harry Tell her, she's got a bloody screw loose.

May Tell him, it's him who's got the screw loose, all their family's alike, they're all bloody barmy.

Paul *slowly turns and walks off stage.* **Annie** *enters during the following.*

Harry At least my family bloody talk. Your father never spoke two words to me.

May What about your father, he didn't know what work was.

Harry At least he was bloody sociable. Your father was a bad pig he treated your mother like shit.

May Don't you talk about my family, you.

Harry You're all bloody barmy.

May Go on, tek off, go on, go . . . I don't ever want to see you again.

Harry I'm going, don't worry.

May I don't know where you're going, nobody's daft enough to bloody have you.

Harry Do you honestly think you'd be able to get rid of me that easy, you foul swine?

May No, I don't. Worse luck.

Annie In nineteen seventy, as a break from the boredom of home, I went away for a few days with our May and Harry. They didn't argue much. We went to Blackpool. We took our Paul, and trailed him around the shops, poor sod. Then I dragged him around the Tower Ballroom. I'm sure our Paul is the clumsiest sod who ever walked a pair of shoes.

Harry   Pit life continued very much the same, except that Mr Poole the under-manager had been killed, and I was working in a face that had two inches of water. The NCB had opened a new social centre which suited me and May, it was just right for dancing.

May   I had my kitchen sink moved into the passage, a lot of folk were having it done, and we were thinking of buying a fridge. Jean Clayworth had got one so I thought it only fair that I should have one. Our Paul seemed to be happy; they said he was above average at his new school.

May, **Annie** *and* **Harry** *exit.*

Kay, *now fourteen years old, runs on stage, followed by* **Paul**, *also fourteen.*

Kay   Catch us then? . . . If you want it . . .

Paul   When I do Kay, I'm gunna get you.

Kay   Gis a kiss then. Come here . . .

Paul   What?

Kay   Yeh . . . there's nobody about.

They force their lips together, a lot of noise.

Paul   Hang on you're breaking my teeth, you're pushing too hard.

Kay   Have I got soft lips?

Paul   Yeh.

Kay   Shall I open my mouth?

Paul   What for?

Kay   French kissing it's called.

Paul   If you want . . .

They kiss, it is sloppy and wet, still very noisy.

Hang on, I'm getting wet all over . . .

Kay   Feel me . . .

Paul   Oh God . . .

Kay   Come on, Paul, feel me . . .

Paul *begins to feel* **Kay**, *about her legs and ribs. A tango is performed.* **Paul** *speaks through it.*

Paul (*to the audience*)   Me and Kay were in the same class at school. There was something about Kay. Every time I got close to her I felt excited . . . every time I was near her, I couldn't leave her alone.

Paul *tries to undo her bra through her jumper.*

Kay   What're you doing?

Paul   Nowt.

Kay   You're squashing me . . . Paul, I can't breathe. I get asthma, Paul . . . What're you trying to do?

Paul   No . . . missed it . . . hang on.

Kay   Do you want me to do it?

Paul   No, hang about, I'll do it.

Kay   Hurry up.

Paul   Oh shit, I'm gerrin cramp in my leg. Oh shit. Bloody hell.

Kay   This is very romantic, I can't breathe, you know?

Paul   Nearly, hang on. Turn around.

Kay   Why?

Paul   Done it.

Kay   Now what are you gunna do?

Kay *runs off.* **Paul** *is left. The lights change.*

His mother and father, with **Aunty Annie**, *enter. It is in every way a domestic scene.* **Annie** *is in washing-up gloves,* **Harry** *sits reading a newspaper.*

May   I want a word with you, me lad.

Paul   What's up?

Harry   Your mother's got a bee in her bonnet.

May   I'll tell you what's up. I thought you said that that mark on your neck was a bruise?

Paul   What mark?

Annie   Leave him, May.

May   No, Annie, I want to get to the bottom of this.

Harry   She'll have her way, Annie.

Annie   He's only doing what's natural.

Harry   She'll drive that lad away from us. You mark my words.

May   Shut up, you!

Harry   Bloody hell.

May   Why didn't you tell us you had a girl-friend?

Paul   Well . . .

May   Are you hiding things from us now. You've been a different lad since you've been to that school.

Paul   No, Mam . . .

Annie   Let him be, May. Look at him, poor sod, he's sweating.

May   What are you doing letting somebody give you a love bite on your neck. Are you thick?

Paul   No, Mam.

May You bloody are.

Harry Leave him now . . .

May I never let your father do that sort of thing to me. Who is she . . . ?

Paul Who?

May You know bloody well who.

Paul Just a lass.

May I want to know who she is . . .

Annie Give it a miss, May, bloody hell.

Paul Kay.

May Kay what?

Paul Cooper, she lives down the other end.

May Right I'm going to see her mam and dad and tell her to stop seeing you.

Paul Mam!

Harry This bloody family.

Annie Poor lad's scared to death.

Paul I don't love her, Mam . . .

May You listen to me.

Harry She'll not give up, she'll not bloody give up until he's crying . . .

Paul Honest, Mam, I don't love her, I never said I did. I'm shakin', I'm scared, Mam . . . Look at me . . .

May You make your mind up, it's me or her, you make your mind up, Paul, because if you see her again, I'm going, I'm off . . . I'm going to pack my bloody bags and go . . .

Paul (*crying*) Mam . . .

May Stop crying, stop it, you're fifteen, now stop it . . .

Annie Calm down, bloody hell calm down . . .

Harry I could bloody belt you for doing that to him, I could . . .

May I bloody love him . . .

Annie Well show it . . .

Paul (*crying*) Aunty Annie . . .

Annie You're bloody setting me off, look at what you're doing. I'm bloody glad that I never had any kids . . . I bloody am.

Tosh, *dressed in seventies school uniform enters upstage and watches the scene before speaking.* **May** *and* **Annie** *exit.*

Tosh Is thy having a game of table tennis?

Paul No I'm stopping in.

Tosh Oh I'll go play by myself then.

Tosh *exits.*

Music plays: 'Volare' then fades slowly. **Paul** *uses the beat of the music to address the audience.*

Paul I never told me mam but I was still seeing Kay, all the way through me exams. And I never told Kay the way me mam was with girls. I don't know what it was but during this time I began to realise that I was going to die, I would lay awake thinking about my own death, and how unfair it was because the world would continue . . . I don't want to die, Dad.

Harry What?

Paul I don't want to die.

Harry Neither do I.

Harry *exits.*

Paul The only thing that made me feel good about dying was that Mark Thompson, the cock of the school, would have to die as well.

The lights change.

Kay *enters wearing clothes she would on her way back from a chocolate factory.*

Kay I'm here, Paul . . .

Paul Kay had left school and had got a job at the chocolate factory. Kay was one of the few things that kept my mind off dying. I would lay in bed at nights and imagine that we were naked together, or imagine that I was rubbing my face between her breasts. Sometimes I even imagined that we were married and had little kids. I wanted to be with Kay for ever.

Kay Are you coming to the Youth Club?

Paul Dunno.

Kay I don't know why I bother going out with you. You're pathetic, you can never come out.

Paul I can. I can do what I want.

Kay You can't, you're tied to t' apron strings.

Paul I'm not. Kiss me.

Kay Is that all you can say? You should leave school, Paul, and come out into the real world. It's brill, I can do what I want. I want a man, you know Paul, not a shirt button.

Paul I've got me exams, ant I?

Kay I might finish with you!

Paul Don't. Kiss me.

Kay For somebody who's supposed to be brainy

you're crap with words, aren't you?

Paul We don't talk to each other in our house, Kay, we just grunt at each other and point like chimps. We don't need words in our house.

Kay What's gunna happen if you go to college?

Paul Nowt . . . Kiss us, Kay . . .

Kay No . . . not here. You sex maniac. I will if you come to the Youthy.

Paul I can't. Me homework.

Kay There isn't such a word as 'can't'. Some lasses at work have been telling me about having it off. They say it's great. Best feeling in the world.

Paul Rather have a laugh, you can have a laugh in Woolies.

Kay They say you should've done it by sixteen. I told 'em about you. I said he's got eight O levels, they said well he should know what to do. Do you wanna do it?

Paul Kiss us . . .

Kay We could do it tonight. Gerrin excited?

Paul Yeh . . .

Kay Do you wanna do it, have it off?

Paul You're too nice . . . just kiss us.

Kay Don't you want it?

Paul *cannot bear it. Music plays: Elvis's 'Fever'.* **Kay** *flaunts. They dance. Out of the night is the voice of* **Aunty Annie**, *sounding like Mother.*

Annie (*off*) Paul?

Paul Shit . . . me mam.

Annie *enters.*

Annie   Hey up, kid!

Paul   Oh hey up, Aunty Annie, I thought it was me mam.

Annie   What you up to then, you bugger?

Paul   Nowt, just talking. This is Kay, Aunty Annie. Me girl-friend . . . I told you about her.

Annie   I know yu' grandma, don't I? Lives just down the road from me. Work at Terry's, don't you? Chocolate factory?

Kay   Yeh, for about six months.

Annie   I used t'work there, mind you it was Blakey's then – seg factory. Eeee, I love them chocolate oranges. Do you make 'em? I love them. Couldn't get us some, could you? I could do with some of them, eh Paul?

Kay   Anyway . . . I'll get off. Might see you down the Youthy later. If you can come down. I'll bring me chocolate oranges for you to look at. Tara.

Kay *leaves.* **Paul** *and* **Annie** *watch her go.*

Annie   That's who all the palaver's over, is it?

Paul   Don't tell me mam, will you?

Annie   You little bugger.

Paul   Don't tell me mam, Aunty Annie, will you?

Annie   No . . . I can keep a secret, kid. I'm good at keeping secrets. Been doing it all my life. You go and enjoy yoursen, eh? Bloody hell . . .

Paul   Gi up Aunty Annie, I'm going red.

Annie   She's a big strapping lass. You go and enjoy yourself while you can. Before old age creeps up on you, and you seize up. I wish I was sixteen and knew what I know now, I do. Go and fly your kite before your nerves get bad like mine. I'm on three different coloured tablets now. Me nerves are shocking. I won't tell your mam, I promise. I can keep a secret.

Annie *exits.*

Paul (*to the audience*)   Me Aunty Annie kept saying her nerves were bad, I should think they were, creeping about like that. She was like a bloody ghost, she drifted about everywhere. Her nerves were bad. At least she lived on her own; she should come and try living in the asylum I laughingly call home. Living in our house was turning me into a nervous wreck.

Blackout. **Paul** *exits.*

Smoke fills the stage. Music plays: 'Ziggy Stardust'. The lights come up.

Tosh, *in full face make-up, enters playing a sweeping brush.* **Paul** *appears, carrying an album cover, a sketch and a tennis racquet.* **Paul** *puts the album cover on a chair and mimes to the music with the tennis racquet.* **Harry** *and* **May** *enter and watch in silence.*

Harry   Bloody hell!

May   What are you two up to?

Paul   Well, just nowt really.

Harry   You're bloody slack the pair on you. What's tha supposed to be, Tosh?

Tosh   Ziggy Stardust and the Spiders from Mars.

May   Does your mam know about this?

Tosh   No, she dun't like Bowie.

Harry   I'm slogging my knackers off at pit . . .

May   Language!

Harry And there's two blokes as big as hosses acting goat miming to records. You're bloody sick. I thought tha wa' supposed to be revising?

Paul I am.

Harry What we got a bloody Martian here for then?

Tosh Just beamed down to get some history books.

Harry Come on, get t' kettle on, mek us a drink.

Paul I'm doing sommat.

May Kettle on . . . now.

Paul Or . . . doing sommat . . .

Tosh I'll have to get off then.

Harry Ar, go and plague somebody else.

Tosh Nice to see you, Mr Hickman. Nice to see Earthlings. I'll get off. I've got another planet to visit. Zig.

Tosh *leaves.* **May** *picks up a sketch done by* **Paul**.

Paul Zog.

May What's this, our Paul? 'Sex creatures from the planet Creedos'?

Paul A level art, Mam.

Harry I bloody wonder about thee.

May I don't understand it.

Harry Tha like a bloody woman. Why don't you get out and get some fresh air. Thy hasn't been wearing make-up, has tha?

Paul No . . . just Tosh . . . He's a laugh, int he.

Harry Ay, bloody hilarious.

Paul (*to the audience*) I don't think me dad appreciated our sense of humour. In fact, I don't know where my humour came from, everybody in our house was always at each other's throats.

Paul *and* **Harry** *exit.* **Annie** *enters, very distraught.*

Annie   I can't cope wi' it, May ... Not any longer I just can't.

May   What's happened?

Annie   That house, it's coming in on me. I can't stay by myself any longer, kid, I'll have to have some company, it's sending me round the twist.

Paul *enters. He is eighteen now.*

Paul   Sup –

Annie   I don't want to upset you, I can't stay there ... I've got to stop somewhere else, May, I've just got to.

May   You can stop wi' us, stop int spare room.

Paul   Brilliant idea that, Mother, where am I gunna revise? We can't swing a cat in this house.

Annie   I don't want to put our Paul off his work, I'll nip down to Roy's mam's; she might be able to see to me.

May   You're stopping here.

Annie   If he's got exams, it's his future.

May   You're stopping here. His dad'll have sommat to say to him, he's not too big to get a clout.

Paul   Sorry, Aunty Annie. I blurted something out, first thing that came into me head.

May   You always do.

Paul   I wonder who I tek after? Sorry, Aunty Annie.

Annie   S'all right, kid.

May It allus happens to this family.

Paul Oh God, she's off now . . .

May It allus happens.

Paul Jesus.

Annie Don't go upsetting yourself.

May I can't help it, everything happens to us. Look at that bloody lot next door, they don't work, four kids, the house is a mess, and all the heartache lands on our doorstep. (*In tears.*) It's not bloody fair.

Paul I'm off out . . .

Paul *leaves.* **Annie** *comforts* **May**.

Annie Hey come on, you're a Parker, aren't you? Don't get upset. Hey, chin up! Happy birthday.

May Oh Annie, you don't know the half of it. I'm worrying myself to death.

Annie What about?

May I'm having such an awful time each month. Harry doesn't know, I've been to the doctor's. He's told me that it's my age. But . . . I mean that's how me mam started.

Annie See a specialist . . . go private.

May I don't like. I don't want our Paul to know I'm not well. He went for an interview to Lancaster and he didn't get in. He's waiting to hear from Sussex now . . . I hope to God he gets in.

Annie That's a long way off.

May He's set his heart and soul on it. I don't want to upset him, but I had to tell somebody, Annie, it's worrying me to death.

Music: 'Moonlight Cocktail'. The lights change.

Paul *enters and watches as* **Annie** *and* **May** *exit. The spotlight picks out* **Paul** *as he slowly walks downstage right. During the following,* **Annie**, **May** *and* **Harry** *stretch out two washing lines and begin hanging up washing – clothing, net curtains, sheets, pillow cases etc. They are only dimly lit.*

Paul   Nineteen seventy-four was like the end of an era for me. Tosh had been kicked out of the sixth form, and then went completely barmy and got a job down the pit. He was working with me dad, which pissed me dad off. But he was only there for two weeks and they were on strike ... which suited Tosh. We started having power cuts and I started getting As for my English essays. We were doing *Sons and Lovers* so that was a doddle for me. Me Auntie Annie was still ghosting about at home, keeping my secret, and forcing me to play Monopoly with her by candlelight. And me mam seemed under the weather but her and me dad still argued and danced and threw food at each other so it couldn't be anything serious. And after six weeks the miners had beaten Ted Heath. Me dad was over the moon and so was Tosh and me mam, so was everybody. Yeh, nineteen seventy-four seemed like a good year to me.

May   I do feel bloody funny.

Harry   She's been washing all day, you can't tell her.

May   I feel bloody awful.

Harry   It'll kill her all this bloody cleaning.

May   What else is there to do?

Annie   It's non-stop washing in this house.

May   I want putting in a bag and shaking up.

Paul   It's true; me mam washed everything. As soon as you took a shirt off your back me mam'd wash it, scrub the collar and have it drying around the fire. She washed towels before they were used, and sheets when I had only slept in them twice. She washed lace curtains four times a week. And our underwear every day. In nineteen seventy-four, I was the cleanest sixth-form student in Europe.

Harry She'll end up wi' arthritis.

Annie She's always got her hands in water.

Harry She'll be bloody crippled when she gets older.

Annie Housework'll be here when she isn't.

Harry It'll get in her bloody bones.

Harry, **Annie** *and* **May** *exit*.

Paul She was obsessed with washing, with cleaning, with the house. We got a new three-piece suite in October nineteen seventy-two, and I swear that she wouldn't let me and me dad sit on it till February nineteen seventy-four. But for all her washing, and ironing, and shouting and bickering and bullying and cleaning and polishing and arguing . . . I loved her.

Paul *exits*.

The lights change. A wind blows very strongly, it is overcast and rain can be heard — it's throwing it down.

May *runs on anxiously. She has a plastic bucket for the washing.*

May Oh bloody hell, look at the bloody weather. Annie? Annie . . . (*She starts to take the washing in.*) Annie . . . Annie!

Annie *runs on.*

Annie Oh hell.

May No rest for the bloody wicked. They said it was gunna be fine.

Annie Where's our Paul?

May   Gone to t' shops. He'll be bloody drenched.

Annie   Look at it, it's like the end of the world.

May   Get 'em off. Don't trail 'em across the floor.

Annie   Shall I tell Mrs Potter next door?

May   You'd better.

Annie (*shouting*)   Mrs Potter? Mrs Potter?

May   Where's Harry? (*Shouting*.) Maggie?

Annie   Usual place.

May   He's always ont bloody toilet.

Annie   I don't think she can hear me, next door.
Maggie . . . Hello! Mrs Potter?

May   I'll never get these buggers dried today. (*She has
her arms full of clothes*.)

Harry *comes out into the rain, pulling up his trousers. He is
holding a letter.*

May   Where've you been?

Harry   Got a letter for our Paul.

May *passes him and exits with the washing and then returns.*
Annie *is still taking the washing off the line.*

Annie   Get some o' these brought in.

Harry   It's from Sussex. Just come . . .

May   Don't get the shirts I'll get them, get the sheets
. . . Don't let 'em trail on the floor.

Paul *enters with* **Tosh**, *they are both fairly wet.*

Paul   Bloody hell. We're soaked.

May   Help your dad.

Tosh   Do you want me to do owt . . . ? Stopped
raining now.

Annie   Bring me the peg-bag.

Tosh   Abandon ship abandon ship, get the washing in . . .

Harry   He's bloody barmy, that lad . . .

May   I'm never gunna get finished today, I'll have t' dry these around the fire.

Harry   Letter for you . . .

May   Don't open it here.

Paul   Why?

May   Can't you wait till you get inside . . .

Paul   I'm opening it.

Annie (*shouting next door*)   Maggie . . . Maggie? Is she bloody deaf next door?

May   Our Annie's more bothered about them next bloody door. Let's get our stuff in, sod 'em.

Tosh *has an armful of clothes.*

Tosh   What shall I do wi' these?

May   Don't crumble 'em up, you silly sod.

Paul *has opened the letter, and is reacting to the news. He has been offered a place to read English at Sussex.*

Annie   It's raining love, your washing's getting wet.

Harry   That's a bloody understatement.

Paul   I've got in. Two Cs and a D. They've offered me. I've got in.

May   Can't you leave that?

Harry   He's got a place . . .

Annie   I've been shouting you for ages . . .

Tosh   Bloody hell, brain-box!

Harry University?

Paul I can't believe it.

Harry Bloody university?

Annie First Hickman to get to university.

Harry Look at me, I'm bloody crying.

Paul I am.

Tosh I am, and I'm not going.

Annie Oh, I'm so pleased for you . . .

Harry I could bloody eat you . . .

Annie I wish me dad could have lived to see him.

May Don't set yourself off.

Annie I do wish he could . . .

Paul Look at us we're bloody three sheets t' wind, we're all soaked.

Tosh It's ruining my hair . . .

Annie Eee, we're proud of you.

May Never mind all this palaver . . . let's get the bloody washing in before we all get pneumonia. Harry put the kettle on, we'll have to celebrate. We'll have a tot of sherry. Tosh come on. Paul bring that line in.

Tosh Hey you can't talk to him like that now you know, he's gunna have letters after his name.

May I'll talk to him how I want, just because he's got in at university doesn't mean he can't help me with the washing. Now come here, bring that bloody line in . . . Bloody university. Bloody hell.

*Harry, **Annie** and **Tosh** exit, followed by **May**. As **May** goes, **Kay** enters, dressed to go out.*

Music plays low: 'Face the Music and Dance'.

Kay   My eighteenth today, or have you forgot? You said you'd come to Tiffany's with me when I was eighteen. Remember? Try and make an effort, Paul, if you think anything about me make an effort . . . It's been three years . . . Come on, Paul!

May *comes out of the house.*

May (*calling loudly*)   Paul, come on, we're all waiting for you!

Silence. **May** *goes.*

Paul *takes his time and looks at* **Kay**, *then slowly he starts to leave her.*

Paul *runs inside to his house.* **Kay** *is left alone. The music plays as the lights fade to —*

Blackout.

Act Two

It is six years later: 1980.

The lights come up on a bare stage. Music plays: 'The Anniversary Waltz'.

May *and* **Harry** *are waltzing together and singing the lyrics to the song. They are both fifty-one.* **Annie** *is also there. She is forty-nine, thin and rather badly worn.*

Harry In nineteen eighty it was me and May's silver wedding anniversary. We celebrated in style at the new Welfare Club.

May All our friends were there. We had a 'bring your own buffet'.

Harry Which meant that everyone brought their own buffet.

May They know that, you sarcastic pig.

Harry May had made some mince pies.

May And there was pie and peas.

Harry Benny Mills had brought some sausage rolls.

May Our Annie had made a trifle.

Harry And Audrey Clarke had made some vol au vents.

May She never made them, they were from Marks and Spencer's.

Annie My trifle was going down well.

May It was everybody's favourite.

Annie I should think it was, I put nearly a full bottle of sherry in it. Tosh has already had three helpings.

Harry Who invited that daft sod?

May   There was Bingo.

Harry   There bloody would be.

May   And a spot waltz. It was smashing.

Harry   It was just what we wanted, not too hectic. If I get excited it sets my chest off.

May   Our Paul had come home especially. Where is he?

Harry   Who?

May   Our Paul?

Harry   Somewhere.

Annie   He's enjoying hissen, he likes to come back up home.

May   He's done well at university. And he said that he came home when he could.

Harry   He's got two degrees. Did his second one part-time.

May   He didn't get a grant so I decided to give him the thousand pounds that me dad'd left.

Harry   We're proud of him.

May   He gets all choked up talking about him.

Harry   I'm proud of him.

May   We've got his cap and gown photo on the mantelpiece.

Annie   I had moved into a smaller house, well it seemed to make sense, didn't it? Took all my old bits and bobs, and threw a lot of stuff out. I've got a loft full of pictures and records, old seventy-eights. Some were our May's.

May   Yes, I want them buggers back.

Annie I worked on an industrial estate for three years, and then did a bit of cleaning up at school . . . I enjoyed that, it was a good gossip.

May I never went to the doctor's.

Harry Their Annie said she should go private.

May I'm going in for some tests. I mean I've been living with this for years. But it's getting bad now. I'm going to see Mr Nish. He's a Pakistani, he's nice. He says I'll feel a different woman when I've had it.

Annie I've told her she won't be a woman, there'll be nowt left.

May She allus looks on the black side.

Harry Twenty-five years!

May Don't mind me.

Harry Twenty-five years.

May And he's never once bought me a red rose.

Harry And it don't seem a day too much . . .

May He's there, our Paul.

Paul *enters. He is twenty-four. Smart, trendy, obviously a student, but smart not hippy.* **Tosh** *is also there. He is the same age, with long hair, maybe back across his face. He is wearing a large leather jacket with a Saxon or Def Leppard T-shirt underneath.*

Tosh Are you dancing?

Paul Not with you.

Tosh How's it going?

Paul Fine.

Tosh Fine?

Paul Don't start telling me that I've changed, Tosh,

or I'll die . . .

Tosh   Thy hasn't lost thee accent then?

Paul (*mocking*)   Eee baar gumm, have I heck.

Tosh   I thought tha might be lah-di-dah!

Paul   Still at t' pit?

Tosh   No, I'm a lawyer now.

Paul   How's me dad doing down t' pit?

Tosh   It's killing him. He thinks he's still twenty-five. Tha wants to get a job down t' pit. It's smashing.

Paul   Touch of irony, eh?

Tosh   I read books and all.

Paul   I know. Will tha get off my back. I'm still the same.

Tosh   Oh ar, I forgot.

Paul   Still into Heavy Metal?

Tosh   No . . . Val Doonican. I've still got all his albums.

Paul   Will tha stop bullshitting?

Tosh   What? Bullshitting, did tha actually say bullshitting? Tha want a pint?

Paul   No, I'll have half.

Tosh   S'up wi' thee?

Paul   Nothing.

Tosh   Have a pint.

Paul   No.

Tosh   Yes.

Paul   No.

Tosh   Tha'll have a pint.

Paul   I don't want one. I'll just have half.

Tosh   I'm not ordering an half in here, they'll think I'm going low.

As they speak **Annie** *walks over bringing a tray of sausage rolls.*

Annie   Here you are, you two, big growing lads. You two buggers. Allus been friends, haven't you? All your lives? Allus been friends, I love you both, I do. Hey, I think that trifle's too alcoholic.

Annie *leaves them.*

Tosh   Be a right bloke have a pint. I can drink ten pints and still drive home.

Paul   I bet I could drink a hundred.

Annie (*to* **May**)   He's with Tosh.

May   They've allus been mates.

Tosh   Tha funny.

Paul   I know.

Tosh   Not funny ha ha, just funny.

Paul   Don't look at me like that, Tosh, I know what you're thinking.

Tosh   Oh tha's a mind-reader and all, is tha?

Paul   I'll have a half.

May, **Harry** *and* **Annie** *form a tableau.*

May   Mr Nish, the consultant, says when I've had it done my nerves won't be half as bad. He says I'll be able to throw the tablets away. Thank God for that; I've been living on 'em for years, there's that many tablets in me, sometimes when I dance you can hear me rattling.

They break the tableau. **Annie** *goes.*

Harry   Come and sit down, you silly bugger.

May   I'm having a great time. Where's our Paul?

Harry   He's with Tosh.

May   They're good mates.

Annie *arrives with a bottle of Bailey's Irish Cream.*

Annie   I've just won a bottle of Bailey's Irish Cream in the raffle.

Kay *enters.* **Paul** *moves across the stage with* **Tosh** *and meets* **Kay**. **Kay** *is twenty-four, very attractive, whorish, stilettoes, over-dressed for the occasion.*

Kay   Oooh, stranger. Your mam's let you come out then?

Paul   Got to be in bed soon though.

Kay   What is it, a lemonade and a wine gum?

Paul   Sommat like that . . . How's it going?

Kay   Married, now, you know. Two kids.

Paul   What's it like? Married life?

Kay   It has its moments.

Tosh   She married Keith Jackson, he works wi' me.

Kay   You look well.

Paul   Good livin'.

Kay   Is there a woman in your life?

Paul   Ish!

Kay   Wedding bells?

Paul   No! Funny, every time I come home I meet somebody who's just got married, or having kids. Next thing you know Tosh'll be married.

Tosh I'm off.

Tosh *moves away.*

Kay I doubt it.

Paul Ouch, you bitch.

Kay I know, aren't I wicked?

Paul You look good. Slimmer.

Kay You allus said nice things.

Paul I meant them.

Kay Made me feel good.

Paul I'm good with words.

Kay Not very good with bra straps though.

Paul I've got better.

Kay Had some practice then?

Paul A bit. Anyway. Nice to see you. Hope the family is OK, say hello to your mam 'n' dad.

Kay I will . . .

Paul Yeh.

Kay See you . . .

Paul Yeh.

She pecks him.

Kay You smell nice . . .

Paul See you . . .

Paul *leaves* **Kay***, she watches him go. He turns, walks to* **Annie***,* **Harry** *and* **May***.*

Annie He's not married, got a career, hasn't he May?

May I was married twenty-five years ago today.

Harry If I'd've killed May instead of marrying her I'd've been a free man ten years ago.

May He's courting. What's she called?

Harry Sommat bloody odd.

Annie What she called, Paul, your girl-friend?

Paul She's not my girl-friend, she's a friend who's a girl. Cherry.

Harry Cherry! Where the bloody hell do they get 'em from?

May We've not met her yet.

Annie We're just telling 'em how well you've done.

Paul Oh yeh.

Annie He's done . . . sommat else, what is it?

Paul An MA. I've had a few years off.

Annie I don't know what the bloody hell it is but it's sommat intelligent.

May He's a bit reserved, is our Paul.

Harry He's like May.

May Hey you, he gets his brains from my side of the family.

Harry Does he, bloody hell!

May He's got it all up here, haven't you, kid?

Paul So they say.

May See.

Paul I'm not sure where they've come from must be all that boiled fish.

May I used to give him boiled fish, me mam swore by it.

Paul I hated it.

May I made him sleep on a board, strengthen his back.

Harry He gets all his talents from me, he gets his moodiness from you.

Annie Yes he does, May, you're moody.

May Oh bloody hell, listen who's talking.

Paul Is everybody OK for a drink?

Annie I'm fine . . . I've had too much I think.

Paul Dad?

Harry No, I'm OK. He fancied himself as a goalie, can you remember?

Paul Oh spare us.

May He thought he was Gordon Banks.

Harry (*calling*) Tosh Tosh . . . come over here.

Tosh What's up, has he bought a pint?

Harry Listen to this.

Tosh *comes over and listens.*

Harry Our Paul fancied himself as a goalkeeper for the local team, and I went to watch him, first time I'd seen him play, and he was jumping about, and he had the gloves and all the bloody rigmorole, and I said to Mr Shaw on the touchline, the bloke who ran the team, I said, what's the score, he says we're losing twenty-four nil, your young 'un's let twenty-four in.

May He let twenty-four in.

Paul I looked brilliant.

Harry I could have buried myself on the touchline.

Paul I was good at diving, I liked to dive.

Harry After the ball had gone in the net.

Paul I don't think it was twenty-four.

Tosh No, more like thirty-four.

Paul (*to the audience*) It was actually seventeen nil. Our family has a tendency to exaggerate.

Harry I don't understand about him having brains. He used to forget whether they were playing at home or away. He once walked all the way to Moorthorpe and when he got there they were playing at Upton.

Paul I only played because you wanted me to, Dad.

Annie I can remember, he used to play in our garage with his Action Man.

Tosh I didn't know thy had an Action Man.

Paul Oh no . . .

Tosh An Action Man? Did it have real hair?

Harry But I'll say this, I only know one other man who's got an MA and that's old Mr Sawyer, headmaster at the grammar school. He's the only other one I know.

Tosh Did it have real hair or plastic hair?

Paul It was bald.

May BA. Bloody Awkward, that's what he's been all his life.

Annie And MA. Moody Article.

Paul Oh my family . . .

Annie I've seen Kay Cooper in here tonight, she's married with two kids. Have you seen her? She looks smashing.

Paul No, I've not seen her.

Harry (*shouting across to someone*)   Tom? Tom, come and meet our Paul. I've told you about him. Come and meet him. We don't see a lot of him . . . Come and meet him . . .

Music: 'Night and Day'.

May   Listen what they're playing, let's get up, Harry.

Harry   I'll get up, what is it?

Annie   'Night and Day'.

May   Come on, Paul, you get up wi' your mam.

Paul   I'd rather not.

Annie   Go on.

May   Come on, you're not that shy.

Harry   Get up with her.

Paul   I can't dance.

May   Follow me, I'll lead, you follow me.

Annie   Course you can dance, anybody can.

Paul   I'm like a board, honest I am.

Annie   Go and dance with your mam.

Paul   No.

Harry   Go on, bloody hell.

Tosh   Go on, Action Man.

Paul   I haven't got a clue what to do.

Tosh   Go on, you fart.

May   Just follow me . . .

Paul *and* **May** *begin to dance.* **May** *dances well but* **Paul** *is clumsy and she takes him around the floor while she sings the entire song. During this, a collage of events takes place:* **Annie** *and* **Harry** *look on and call out to* **Paul**; **Tosh** *laughs and,* *upstage left in a pose,* **Kay** *stands with the wind machine lifting her skirt, showing her legs in suspenders;* **Paul** *cannot help but look at* **Kay**. *Altogether, it's a nightmarish vision.*

Annie   He's as stiff as a board, drag him around, May.

Harry   He's made sommat for hissen.

Tosh   Go on, Paul . . . go on.

Annie   He's got worse since Blackpool.

Kay   Smile, Paul, relax and smile.

Harry   Don't watch your feet.

Kay   Ring me up, Paul, I'm in the book give me a ring, I'm under Jackson, K. Jackson.

Harry   He's gerring it.

Annie   I think he was better at football.

The cast, with the exception of **May** *and* **Paul**, *sing along with the record.*

Annie, **May**, **Harry** *and* **Tosh** *exit, clearing all items from the stage.*

The music fades. The lights crossfade to give an outdoor night effect. **Paul** *and* **Kay** *are outside in the car park.*

Kay   We didn't have much time to talk in there, did we?

Paul   No, not really.

Kay   How long are you staying up at home for?

Paul   Not long if I can help it.

Kay   Oh.

Paul   Where's the husband?

Kay   Tosh's had to take him back. He drinks too much.

Paul   So you're all on your own?

Kay   'Fraid so. We should have a chat, you know, Paul. About the old times. We had some laughs.

Paul   We did.

Kay   I'll never forget the things we used t' get up to. The pictures are very clear in my mind.

Paul   Indelibly inked?

Kay   If you say so. You know, I feel like I know you but you seem like a complete stranger.

Paul   You look lovely, Kay. I could eat you.

Kay   I've got all the right bumps that's all.

Paul   I better get off home.

Kay   I thought you might have lost your accent.

Paul   I've lost everything but . . . How are you getting home?

Kay   Walk.

Paul   Give you a lift if you want?

Kay   Got a car?

Paul   Second-hand Allegro.

Kay   Can I trust you, Paul? Just me and you in a car, we've got a history, you know?

Paul *and* **Kay** *exit.*

Music: 'Night and Day'. The lights change, the music fades, it is the next morning.

Paul, **May** *and* **Harry** *enter, with chairs.* **May** *has a newspaper.*

May   We had a great night, didn't we, we had a good night.

Harry We did.

May What time did you get in? I was still awake at half-twelve and there was no sign of you. What were you up to?

Paul Went round to Tosh's.

Harry Told you.

May That's what your dad said.

Harry Have a good night?

Paul Yeh.

May It was a good night. Our Annie enjoyed it, I think she was drunk.

Harry No wonder with that bloody trifle.

May I've got me Bingo to do. Three numbers, I only want three numbers.

Harry There's probably another three thousand people all wanting three numbers. Anybody want a cuppa?

Paul I don't know why you read that paper.

Harry It's your mother.

May I like to do the Bingo.

Paul It's mindless.

May Forty thousand you can win. I don't think that's mindless. A woman in Rotherham won it last week, it's getting nearer.

Harry Your mother and Bingo!

Paul It wants burning.

May I read the stars and do the Bingo that's all I read in it, I don't look at page three, and then we use it to start the fire.

Harry Cartoons are the best thing in it.

May What are you gunna have for your dinner?

Paul What is there?

May Cheese and egg, like you like it, or fry up. Or cold ham and some sausage rolls.

Paul What else is there?

May I thought you liked cheese and egg?

Paul I did. I might have Chinese, skip dinner have something later.

May What do you want a Chinese for?

Paul Because I like it.

May It's rubbish to me.

Paul (*indicating the newspaper*) So is that. But you still read it.

Harry Look out.

May What is it that you say about us? Chops with everything, he says we have chops with everything.

Paul Chips, Mother, chips. It's a play.

May We don't have chips with everything. We don't have chips with cheese and egg, do we Harry?

Harry No, and we don't have chips with chips.

May We have tea with everything.

May *hits* **Paul** *with the paper and then she exits.*

The lights change.

Paul (*addressing the audience*) I could just about stand it at home for a day; it was worse than being in San Quentin. My every move was monitored by me mother, I could actually see the walls of the house getting bigger and bigger, trapping me with them. So I

would make some feeble excuse about having to go
back to London to go to the library or to see Cherry.

The lights change.

May *enters with a dustpan and brush.* **Paul** *is about to leave.*

May Are you going?

Paul I can't work at home any more, Mam.

May I've bought you some of that packaged Chinese
stuff, I thought you liked it.

The lights change. **May** *is sweeping the floor.*

Paul (*to the audience*) And I would leave with a lump
in my throat. And as I left I would see my mother
sweeping the carpet, sweeping every little speck of dust
from the carpet, every piece of toast that dropped on
that carpet made a sound to her like a bomb going off
... I saw the veins in her knarled hands grasping at
the Beta-ware ... It was her life, her creativity,
'cleanliness is next to godliness', she would say, and I
left with a real sense of freedom and breath of fresh
air, and I left them with whatever problems they had.
She never heard my goodbye, she was still sweeping
the carpet.

Paul *leaves. As he does* **Mrs Potter** *and* **Annie** *stand in
spotlights.* **Harry** *despairs at* **May**.

Mrs Potter She's having it done then.

Annie What?

Mrs Potter The operation? When's she go in?

Annie About a month.

Mrs Potter Well tell her if she's in need of anything
while she's in, to give me a shout.

Annie I'll tell her.

Mrs Potter I know we haven't always got on, but if

she wants helping out she knows where I am.

Annie   Thanks.

Mrs Potter   The sister-in-law had it done. Knocked her up and all very bad. She was never the same again. Knocks the stuffin' out of you so they say.

Mrs Potter *exits*.

Annie (*to the audience*)   Everyone had our May's operation on their minds but no one spoke of it. I busied myself by cleaning out the loft and putting all my seventy-eights into boxes. I thought I'd give them to her when she came out.

Harry   She'll be all right once she's been in.

Annie   She decided to decorate the house before she went in, so as it would be spick and span when she came out. She wallpapered from top to bottom.

Harry   She's going round the bloody bend.

Annie   I told her she was barmy.

Harry   You can tell her but she doesn't bloody listen.

Music: Doris Day singing 'Que Sera Sera'.

Harry, **May** *and* **Annie** *leave*.

The lights change. **Paul** *takes a seat downstage left. During the following, a hospital bed is brought on upstage left and* **May** *enters and gets into the bed.*

Paul (*to the audience*)   Deep down I knew it was a chance to see Kay again so . . . I dragged myself back up home for six days when me mam had her hysterectomy. Apparently there was something malignant inside her, and this should sort it out. I hate going to hospitals they make me feel ill . . . It was the first time in twenty-seven years that me dad had been left in the house on his own. He was lost, utterly. He'd come home from work, breathless, and wheezing and sit for three hours on the backstep chopping firewood. He chopped enough firewood to keep the entire Western civilisation in firewood for the next fifty years. Then he would dust around the house, listing things as he did them: 'the brasses', 'the window ledges', 'wash the lino'. Whenever he spoke he sounded like me mother, she had him well trained. And then at night we'd sit by the fire, and like Beckett and James Joyce we'd exchange silences . . . All the while I kept thinking, this man is my dad . . . He would tell me about the 'good old days' about the great times he and me mam had had together, he loved me mam so much, but for some reason he never ever told her . . .

During the following, while **Paul** *continues to speak to the audience,* **May** *is wheeled centre. The lights are still dark.*

Paul (*slowly walking over to the bed*) When we went to see her she looked like a piece of meat, like a dead pig on a slab all dressed in pink. She was still under the anaesthetic.

The lights change. **May** *is asleep.*

Paul (*to* **May**) Brought some Lucozade. More goodness in one orange so they say. One pound ten for that . . . And some grapes. Me dad's parking the car. Should be here in an hour. You all right? . . . Asleep.

Paul *grabs a chair, sits at the foot of the bed, looks around, eats some of his mother's grapes, and then has a drink of Lucozade.* **Harry** *comes in.*

Paul Asleep.

Harry Oh. Still under.

Harry *sits next to* **Paul** *at the foot of the bed.*

Paul Wanna grape?

Harry Do you think she'll be all right?

Paul Yeh.

Harry Good. Smells funny, doesn't it?

Paul Good view though.

Silence.

Harry We don't often get time to talk, do we?

Paul Not often.

Harry You know, I don't understand what it is that you do.

Paul I write reviews, articles for magazines – films, music – try and flog 'em. I get expenses.

Harry Sounds interesting.

Paul And I sign on.

Harry You're not wasting a good education then?

Paul Was that supposed to be a joke?

Harry How's Cherry?

Paul On and off at the moment.

Harry Are we ever gunna see her?

Paul Dunno. Another grape?

Silence.

Harry Weather's smashing for November.

Paul Snow forecast.

Harry Is it?

Paul According to the radio.

Harry Oh dear.

Paul She'll need to rest when she comes out. She's never done anything interesting, has she?

Harry Everything's ready for her when she gets

back.

Paul Another grape?

Harry You can go, you know, if you want. You don't have to stop here. I mean if you've got sommat to do.

Paul I'm fine.

Harry There's another hour.

Paul No . . . it's nice and warm.

Harry She'll be all right.

Paul Yeh.

Harry Tough as old boots.

Paul She works too hard. Never relaxes.

Harry Thanks for cooking. I'm useless. That Italian thing was lovely. I've never had that before, what was it?

Paul Tagliatelle.

Harry Smashing that.

Paul Yeh?

Harry Yeh.

Paul I saw it in the dustbin, Dad, I saw that you'd thrown it in the dustbin.

Harry Not all of it.

Blackout. Music: 'Blue Tango', during which the hospital bed is struck.

May *and* **Harry** *exit.* **Kay** *appears in a spotlight wearing a fetching red dress.*

Kay (*to the audience*) Yeh I'm happy, aren't I, I'm satisfied. I've got two little kids and a husband who knocks me about. I've got a mortgage and a microwave, I'm happy. I mean it, very happy. But I'm not excited, not any more, I feel like I've done all there is to do, my life is over. I don't feel nervous any more, like something special is going to happen, that's been taken out of me, the boredom, the nappies, the routine, has beaten that out of me. So it was a strange thing, but I knew it was going to happen sooner or later ... I could feel excitement running through my veins again. He was my hero, my very own Milk Tray man, I knew that I was looking at him through a soft focus, I'm not that stupid ... but I had to have him. I wanted to eat him. He was like a big red shiny apple, fresh and unspoilt and I wanted to sink my teeth into his flesh, I wanted to bite him, and I wanted him to want me. He was a big, red rosy apple and I wanted to eat him ... We met in the pub on Wednesday, Keith was on afters.

The lights change.

Paul   She seemed extra-special now, she seemed to be more of a woman ... I couldn't help myself, she cast this web over me. Christ, I talk such bullshit.

Kay   Keith would have killed us both if he ever found out but it seemed to be the most wicked thing in the world.

Paul   I'd been at the hospital all day.

Kay   We had a few drinks ... I had to know.

Paul   It was like being caught in an avalanche.

Kay   Very cramped and sweaty.

Paul   In the back of an Allegro.

Kay *and* **Paul** *tango upstage behind the set. We hear comic orgasmic noises. Suddenly,* **Paul** *appears, holding his back.* **Kay** *follows him.*

Paul   Oh me back. I've got cramp in me back.

Kay Are you OK?

Paul Yeh. Sorry. Sorry, Kay.

Kay Well, was it what you expected?

Paul Fourteen years I've dreamt of that, Kay, and now? Sorry. I should never have done it. I feel awful.

Kay Not as awful as me, I got me leg stuck.

Paul Oh, what have I done. You shouldn't have led me on, Kay.

Kay It takes two to tango.

Paul I shouldn't have ever seen you again, I shouldn't have . . . I've got no will-power.

Kay You could have said no, Paul, you could have gone home.

Paul In a car, in the back of a car? Oh my God.

Kay Stop being so bloody melodramatic. It was just a passing moment. I don't love you, Paul, but I had to have one moment's excitement.

Paul But that's the point, Kay.

Kay What is? What are you on about?

Paul I love you.

Kay Rubbish!

Paul I do, I always have. You've always been in my head.

Kay Paul? Don't!

Paul I mean it. God, I mean it. I can't get rid of you. You're there, haunting me all the time. Oh, it shouldn't have been like this, Kay.

Kay It didn't mean anything.

Paul I can't ever see you again!

Kay Don't flatter yourself. I love my family, Paul. I love 'em, this was just an electric shock to remind me that I'm still alive.

Paul I should never have done it.

Kay Don't worry about it, Paul. You'll get over it. I got over you . . .

Paul I was so pathetic.

Kay You were OK given the circumstances.

Paul Don't tell anybody, Kay. Please?

Kay Don't worry I'm not likely to tell your mam, am I?

Paul I'm sorry . . . I should never have done it.

Kay Come on, we'll get some fish and chips, make a night of it.

Blackout. Music: 'Bali Hai'.

Paul *and* **Kay** *exit.* **May** *and* **Annie** *enter.*

The lights come up. **Annie** *is smoking.* **May** *is highly-strung and nervous.*

Annie Fancy striking. He should go back to work. What are you going to live on? It's every man Jack for hissen. I bet them union leaders are getting sommat.

May Harry's allus stood by the union. He'll not change now.

Annie They want shooting, all them bloody pickets. They're stopping decent blokes from working.

May For God's sake put a sock in it.

Annie Look at you, it's getting you down again is this strike, you'll end up in hospital again.

May Just shut up, our Annie, before you go too far.

Annie   Police are only doing their jobs.

May   He says he's not crossing that line, he says, he'll join 'em. He's not working. I don't care if it makes me badly, he's not working. We can't let her beat us, she can't beat the Yorkshire miners, never will she. Me dad stood by the union and Harry is.

Annie   She'll beat 'em, you daft sod, she's got a bloody plan.

May   They'll all come out, all of 'em. They'll all come out and support the Yorkshire miners, she'll never beat them buggers, not as long as she's got an hole in her arse . . .

Annie   It's on telly, you can see 'em all causing trouble.

May   They don't show it all.

Annie   I could throw stones at the pickets.

May   And I'll throw stones through your bloody windows. I didn't vote for 'em.

Annie   I did.

May   You voted for that bloody lot?

Annie   I bloody did, Labour's never done owt for me.

May   Get out of this house.

Annie   It'll go on for ever this strike.

May   Get out, Annie.

Annie   You'll make yourself bad again.

May   I don't care!

Annie   Do you think they'll win? You're livin' in a bloody dream world.

May   Annie, get out of this bloody house. You're a silly sod, never vote for thcm, ever, whatever happens, never, me dad told me that. He lost his bloody lungs down the soddin' pit. Get out, Annie, I mean it.

Annie   You'll finish up in Stanley Royd, you will.

May   Get out.

Annie   You're just like me dad, three sheets to t' wind.

May   I don't want to talk to you.

Annie   You drive 'em all away. Our Paul dunt come home like he should because of your bloody tantrums. You're bloody evil, if you'd 've treated him like a proper lad he'd think more of you . . . Where is he when you want him?

May   Don't you bloody talk to me about kids. You don't know what it's bloody like. You should have had some kids when you had a chance instead of thinking you and Roy were Lord and Lady Muck.

Annie   I hope this strike lasts for ever, I do. I hope you never have any money, and don't be coming to me for a bloody hand-out because my door will be shut.

May   I'll have all the bloody things back from me mam's that you've been hoarding and all.

Annie   Well, you'll have to come and get 'em then. Because I'm not bringing 'em up here. I'll not come up here again until you're dead.

May   You're a bloody worm, Annie Parker, get out of my sight.

Annie   You're evil you are. Evil.

May *and* **Annie** *are in tears. Blackout.*

May *and* **Annie** *exit.* **Mrs Potter** *enters carrying a placard which reads* 'COAL NOT DOLE', **Tosh** *and* **Harry** *stand upstage.*

The lights come up.

Tosh   Come January we'd been out nearly a year.

Mrs Potter   Leave 'em alone, you bullies.

Harry   We're fighting for us jobs, you silly sods.

Mrs Potter   They're not from round here, them police.

Tosh   Shit for brains.

Harry   Get a PROPER JOB.

Tosh   I'll bite your head off, you wimps. Humour was a bit thin on the ground.

Mrs Potter   You bloody puppets.

Tosh   We built three snowmen outside the pit gates.

Harry   We put bits of coal for eyes and nose.

Mrs Potter   The police sat there in their Range Rover looking at 'em smiling.

Tosh   One of 'em says, is it your own work? I says yeh.

Mrs Potter   And then the police ran into our snowmen. You bullies.

Harry   Smashed down the end one.

Tosh   I called him Derek.

Harry   Smashed down the other one.

Tosh   That was his wife, Doreen.

Mrs Potter   They they smashed into the middle one. He was the son. We called him Paul.

Harry   And the Range Rover stopped, they jolted forward in their seats.

Mrs Potter   You're not smiling now.

Tosh We'd built the middle 'un around a concrete post. You bastards.

Mrs Potter They'll never go back.

Harry She'll never shut Kirkby pit.

Tosh There's two hundred years of coal down there.

Mrs Potter How much are you getting in overtime?

Harry She'll never shut Kirkby.

Tosh Why don't you get a man's job. Yes, come on, pal, just me and you. I'm six feet ten of insanity.

Mrs Potter Get back down south.

Harry She'll never shut Kirkby.

Music: 'Moonlight Serenade'. The lights fade slowly to a spotlight on **Paul** *who walks slowly downstage right to address the audience.*

Harry, **Tosh** *and* **Mrs Potter** *exit.* **May** *enters during the following.*

Paul (*to the audience*) I knew sooner or later that things would come to a head wi mam and dad. I felt like I was betraying myself if they didn't. I didn't come home all year during the miners' strike, I couldn't face the obscenity of it, they'd been ripped apart. And I couldn't run the risk of seeing Kay. So I phoned and listened to me mam talk nonsense about politics, and me dad get all worked up in the background. I made the mistake of telling them I was playing in a pub band, I was livin' with Cherry, and I didn't have a 'proper job'. As far as me mam and dad were concerned I was now a Martian.

The lights change.

May When are we gunna see her then?

Paul Who?

May   Sherry. You hardly come home as it is.

Paul   Cherry.

May   Three years now, we don't know a thing about her. Is she black, white, red, green? Where's she from, what's she like?

Paul   She's all those things and more.

May   I wonder about you sometimes, you're mucky, you smell, you never look smart. I didn't bring you up not to have a shave. I thought when you came she could have come, let us have a look at her.

Harry *enters from the kitchen. He is older, slower.*

Harry   Bloody Cherry, what sort of name is that?

May   I bet he takes bloody drugs.

Paul   This is why I don't ask her up.

May   Why what's up with us?

Harry (*with a sense of irony*)   There's nowt wrong wi rate folks.

Paul *is exasperated by his parents.*

Paul (*starting to move into gear*)   You two, it's like Torquemada, it's like the bloody Inquisition. You want to know everything, and when you find out all you do is criticise.

May   You've never told us about her.

Paul   I've never been able to. I can't talk to you about myself, to you I'm an object. I know you worship me, but I've never felt like a person with you and me dad, only ever in my head.

May   You can talk to us about anything.

Harry   We're broadminded, me and your mam.

Paul   I can't, that's where you're wrong.

May   Oh we're wrong again.

Paul   See?

May   Wrong again.

Harry   I'm bloody fed up of being wrong. I was wrong for supporting Scargill, according to you, I was wrong not eating Italian shite, I was wrong for making you play football, you're the one who's wrong, you're the one who's not got a bloody job, and six years at bloody college, while I've been coughing me knackers up –

May   Hey, steady . . .

Harry   – I bet there isn't a more educated bloke at the soddin' dole office.

Paul   I've got a job. I'm doing what I want to do.

May   He's a disgrace.

Paul   Jesus . . . You're so limited.

May   Stop swearing in this house, this is my house, I don't want any bloody swearing.

Harry   That's all they do that lot, bloody swear.

May   He's a disgrace.

Paul   I'm twenty-eight years old, I do what I want!

May   You look a bugger.

Harry   I'm ashamed of him, I am. Ashamed of him.

Paul   God help us!

May   I'll tell you why we haven't seen her, this bloody Cherry.

Paul   Go on then, know-all, go on then, tell us why?

May   Because he's ashamed of where he comes from.

Paul   Don't talk rubbish.

May He is.

Paul Mother, you talk bloody rubbish.

Harry You're a bloody wash-out.

May You mark my words, he's afraid we'll show him up, get in his way, like he said we did at that graduation. Well I'll tell you sommat: I didn't want to go and stand about with that bloody type anyway, set o' bloody farts.

Harry They're pathetic that lot. Set o' bloody snobs.

May We're not good enough for her.

Paul *is bursting. He half means this.*

Paul All right, yes, I don't bring her home because I'm ashamed: because every time I come into this bloody house, there's arguing, and I can't sit on that, or have I got clean on? or I've dropped a crumb, are my socks clean, have I had a shave today? And you two are at each other's throats all the time. Do you honestly think everybody in the world shouts at each other all the time, do you, honestly? Do you think reasonable conversation is dead? That because somebody has a different opinion to you, Mother, it makes them less of a person. Do you –

May Look at him shouting.

Paul I'm shouting to make sure you hear me, because we are now on different planets, I'm on Mars and you two are on bloody Pluto.

Harry Stop swearing at your mother.

Paul And why should I bring somebody somewhere where they aren't wanted. Now . . . That's it. I've finished. I've had my say. Sorry. But . . . I had to say it. Sorry.

Silence.

May   Well, if that's how you feel about us you had better leave, and not come back.

Paul   Jesus, this is a nut-house, I can't talk rationally to you. I was just getting it off my chest.

May   And I'm getting this off mine, let him go.

Paul   I will.

May   Go.

Paul   I will.

May   Go. Get.

Paul   If I walk out of here, you'll never see me. I'll never come back, I swear to God.

May   Go.

Harry   There's no need for all this upset.

Paul   I mean it, Mother.

May   And I bloody mean it, you're dealing with your mother here, not some shit-arse from university. If that's the way you feel, go. Get out.

Harry   I said this would happen.

May   It's you and all, not just me, he's talking about, you and all. Let him go!

Silence.

Paul   Right.

Paul *leaves. Silence.*

Harry (*in an outburst, through tears*)   I could kill you, I could, I could kill you. Oh God . . . that's my lad . . . My lad . . . I could swing for you . . .

May   Let him go . . .

Harry   This family. This bloody rotten family.

They freeze. Silence. The lights change.

Annie *enters.*

Annie (*to the audience*)   Our May had got me dad's streak in her; she didn't mind hurting people even if it meant hurting herself. She never wanted our Paul to leave like that.

May   He can go, I'm not bothered what he does.

Annie   She turned the hurt in on herself, like someone pulling their own teeth, she enjoyed the agony. She let it fester inside her. Arguing with our Paul must have torn her up inside, he was all she lived for.

May   He never rings me these days.

Annie   I never saw her, I stayed at home and knitted and on a weekend I'd still go and keep Roy's grave nice and tidy. I'd often see Kay Cooper, she'd had another little boy . . . and was looking well.

Annie *exits.*

The lights change. Music: 'April in Paris'. **Harry** *and* **May** *address the audience.*

Harry   In nineteen eighty-six we went to Paris. We went on a bus trip.

May   Paris was breathtaking.

Harry   We saw everything, the Arch de Triumph, Louvre.

May   We walked by the Seine.

Harry   I was nearly in seine.

May   That's supposed to be a joke.

Harry   Bonjour, May.

May   Bonjour, Harry.

Harry   We picked up a bit of French.

May   Bloody hell!

Harry   We bought French bread.

May   We saw the *Mona Lisa.*

Harry   I saw the moaner May.

May   Pathetic, he is, he's pathetic with jokes.

Harry   And wished I'd taken redundancy ten years ago. We had fifteen thousand. By the time we'd paid for the house there wasn't much left; but I felt free, I felt like I'd got the sun on my back. I felt twenty years younger. We walked all over Paris, made ourselves bad with it.

May   My arthritis was bad. But it was a time for getting to know each other again.

A burst of 'April in Paris'.

May *and* **Harry** *exit. Then they return:* **Harry** *with an ironing board and iron.* **May** *with a sheet, and they begin to attempt to fold the sheet.*

Harry   We were like little kids. I missed the pit like a hole in the head.

May   He's a liar . . . for the first year he never stopped talking about the pit; at night he'd be sat up in bed wide awake waiting for the shift to start.

Harry   We worked as a team on the domestic front. I used t' say that May lets me make all the big decisions, like will we have nuclear fuel, or should we be in the Common Market, and I let her make all the small decisions, like where are we going for our holidays or how much are we gunna spend at the supermarket. (*He begins to iron.*)

May   I never saw our Annie, there was just the two of us. And we hardly went out.

Harry I started to potter about the house doing DIY. I became an expert. I could build a wardrobe in a telephone box, and May would have made a great under-manager; she had me working harder than Mr Poole ever did. Have you had a tablet?

May I'll tek one.

Harry You should have one after every meal it says on the packet.

May Do you allus do everything you're supposed to?

Harry No.

May Well then.

Harry Oh, that's OK then.

May Iron the corners.

Harry I am.

May You're not.

Harry I am.

May I can see from here that you're not.

Harry Do you want to iron 'em?

May No, me hands are bad . . .

Harry Well shut up then, moan-a-lot.

May That's told me.

Harry Put a record on.

May You put one on.

Harry Only if you smile, you foul pig, who do you want?

May Glen Miller. I'm smiling.

Music: 'Elmer's Tune'.

Harry *exits with the ironing board and iron.* **May** *clears the* *chairs.* **Harry** *returns with a lawn-mower.* **Tosh** *enters and sees him.*

Tosh Get that grass cut.

Harry Na then.

Tosh How's retirement, tha like it?

Harry Fantastic. If I had my time agen I'd be a gardener.

Tosh I thought tha got hayfever?

Harry That's the only drawback. How's things going down at work?

Tosh Tha hasn't heard then?

Harry Heard what?

Tosh She's shuttin' Kirkby pit.

Harry Give over.

Tosh They've given us an offer, take the money or a job at another pit. Well, that makes sense, dun't it, in a shrinking industry? All the best jobs have gone.

Harry When's she shuttin' it?

Tosh A fortnight.

Harry Well, they might shut the Welfare an' all, tha knows, social money came from t' pit into the Welfare . . . be no dancin' then.

Tosh Ar. Bastards. Ninety-five per cent of what Scargill said was right.

Harry What's tha gunna do?

Tosh Dunno.

Harry Bloody hell, she's shutting Kirkby. (*He sneezes.*)

Tosh Bless you.

Harry Thanks.

Tosh I might start a window-cleaning job, tha knows, set me own firm up.

Harry Well there's one thing, you won't need a ladder.

Tosh I'll need a bucket though.

Harry Fifty years ago they were crying out for miners. Essential works order, now we're on the scrap-heap. Your young lads'll not get much.

Tosh No, I might go and see Bruce Springsteen with my redundancy money.

Harry Hey Tosh ... I feel right sorry for you.

Tosh Ar ... I do. How's laddo?

Harry We never hear from him from one week to the next.

Tosh Ar well ... Cut your grass for a fiver.

Harry Bugger off.

Tosh I mean it.

Harry Is tha joking?

Tosh No ...

Harry Go on then.

Tosh *takes the mower and exits.*

The scene changes to **Harry** *and* **May**'*s home. It is 1988, and it is* **May**'*s sixtieth birthday.*

Harry *fetches some chairs.* **May** *enters. She looks much older and she is wearing slippers and a cardigan over her dress.*

May Sixty?

Harry Sixty ...

May   Bloody sixty not out. Where's my red roses?

Harry   Still in the shop.

May   Ay I thought they would be. You're about as romantic as a woodlouse. Never bought me any flowers.

Harry   They give me hayfever, you know that.

May   Never bought me any.

Harry   Bloody sixty.

May   And achieved bloody nowt. It all seems to have gone by so quickly. I could roar when I think about it. And I thought we were going to be the folks who lived on the hill.

Harry   That was going to be Annie and Roy.

May   Arr ... poor old Roy. I wonder what he'd 've been doing now? Sixty? Nowt to look forward to.

Harry   We're going away next year, bus trip to Paris.

May   I love Paris, sommat about it. I love it.

Harry   You're only as old as you feel.

May   Nowt to look forward to, it's all behind us now.

Harry   We could go into home improvements. You could go around checking up to see if people are cleaning their houses good enough.

May   I don't clean my own like I did.

Harry   You do too much.

May   Bloody sixty, and I've only got two cards.

Harry   One better than last year. (*He takes a moment and then addresses the audience.*) She's not been too well, to be honest. I think the doctors thought that the operation would catch it, but I don't think it has. She's in terrible pain sometimes. We haven't told anybody.

And me? Sometimes I look in the mirror and wonder who I am.

Tosh *enters still dressed as for a rock concert. He is carrying a bottle of Remy Martin with the price still on it.*

Tosh   Can I come in? Na then?

May   Hey up Tosh, come in, lad.

Tosh   Harry!

Harry   All right?

Tosh   Happy birthday, Mrs H. (*He hands her the bottle of Remy Martin.*)

May   Oh Tosh ... oh, you shouldn't have.

Tosh   It's rate.

May   A bottle of brandy, Remy Martin. Int that nice, you've left the price on ...

Harry   Thought that counts.

Tosh   It's to share really.

May   Look at the price, you shouldn't have.

Tosh   Care of Mr Sainsbury that. I didn't buy it, he'll not miss one bottle.

May   Oh, you little bugger.

Tosh   Sixty then? What's it feel like?

May   Old.

Harry   Fantastic.

Tosh   Me mam's seventy-one in August.

Harry   Ar?

May   Seventy-one.

Tosh   I thought I'd pop round, nowt else to do.

May You can do my windows if you like, while you're here.

Tosh It'll cost you. I'm self-employed now, you know, I don't do owt for nowt.

Paul *and* **Cherry** *(dressed in a Laura Ashley print) appear at the door. Silence. Everyone is very tense throughout the following scene.*

Paul Can I come in or what?

Harry Bloody hell!

Cherry *(shyly)* Hello.

Paul Happy birthday, Mam. Have I got the right day?

May What do you want? There's nowt here for you.

Paul I thought this was 'home'?

May I thought you were never coming back?

Paul I wasn't.

May Well, what you come for? You're ashamed of us, aren't you?

Harry Give it a miss, May.

May We could be dead for all he's bothered.

Paul Can we come in or what?

Harry Ar bloody hell, get yourselves in.

May Well look at you, you look like a bloody circus. Have you got clean on?

Paul Mother spare us. Tosh?

Tosh Not bad.

Paul Zig?

Tosh Zog.

They shake hands.

May   Who is this then?

Paul   Mam, this is Cherry.

Tosh   Cherry?

Cherry   Paul's told me all about you, Mrs Hickman.

May   I bet he has an' all.

Tosh   What sort of bloody name is that?

May   I bet he's told you what a bad pig I've been to him.

Cherry   Well, no . . . not really.

May   Everything we did, we did for him; everything we sacrificed, we sacrificed for him; and then he turned his bloody back on us.

Paul   Here, happy birthday. Don't say I never give you owt.

May   I don't want anything off you.

Paul   Bloody tek it. (*He offers her a rose and a wrapped present: Chanel No. 5.*)

Harry   Cuppa tea, anybody? May? Cherry? Cuppa tea. I'm allus making tea, Cherry, I mek more tea than Typhoo.

Cherry   Yes, please, Mr Hickman . . . It's a nice house, Mrs Hickman.

Harry *exits.*

May   It should be, all I do is clean it. It should be more than nice.

Cherry   I like the wallpaper.

May   Blown vinyl, I got it in Wakefield. Oh Chanel No. 5, Harry. He must think we stink, and a red rose.

Bloody hell. I've had to wait sixty years for that.

Paul   I heard about Kirkby. Out of work?

Tosh   No, I'm a brain-surgeon now.

Paul   Well, you've got the hands for it.

May   I'm surprised you remembered where we live.

Cherry   We called a month ago.

Paul   Nobody in.

Harry *enters from the kitchen.*

Harry   We've been away, Yugoslavia. Only cheap. I've got a jar in there, Paul, and I can save seventy quid in it in twenty pence pieces. Every time I get one I put it in me jar. It's me 'going-away jar'.

Paul   Sounds good.

Harry   Ay . . . Shall I get a bit of cake out, May?

Tosh   Ay, get some cherry cake. Soz, couldn't resist that one.

May   Has she met Tosh?

Tosh   Is that your real name?

Cherry   Is Tosh yours?

Tosh   No it's Edward, but I feel a bit of a fart being called Edward around here.

May   He's all rate, aren't you, Tosh?

Paul   Don't bother with any food, Dad. I thought we'd go out, I've made arrangements for us all to go out.

May   I'm not going out.

Cherry   We've booked a table.

May   I'm stopping in.

Paul   Mother . . . ?

Harry   Come on, May . . . he's treating us.

May   No, I don't want to go out.

Harry   She hardly ever goes out. She's like a fixture, you can't get her out of the house. She just sits and listens to the wireless.

May   Shut up, you.

Cherry   You'll enjoy it, Mrs Hickman.

May   How do you know if I'll enjoy it?

Cherry   Well . . . I thought . . .

Harry   Come on, May . . .

May   No . . . I've told you.

Paul (*making an effort*)   Come on, you foul old swine. I've booked for a carvery, now come on. Get ready, let's go out and have a good birthday.

May   No . . . I'm not going out. I'm not going. I'm staying in this house, this is my house, I'm staying in it. Don't think you can come and start ordering me about. I'm not going anywhere, I'm not.

Harry   May?

May, *in tears, begins to make her way out.* **Tosh** *stands up.*

May   No, I didn't ask him to come back – he can go back to London for me. Go back where he bloody belongs.

Harry *is about to follow her off. The atmosphere is difficult.* **May** *exits.*

Harry   She gets all upset, she's not well. She's pleased to see you.

Harry *exits.*

Tosh   Anyway ... I'll get off. Just popped around to see 'em. I keep me eye on 'em. Funny how things work out, int it? Kay's left her husband, tha knows? Lives with her mam.

Paul   No, I didn't know.

Tosh   Anyway. Nice to meet you, Cherry. Cheers. I'll get off home, make me mam a cuppa.

Tosh *leaves.* **Cherry** *and* **Paul** *are left alone.*

Cherry   Is your mum OK?

Paul   I told you we shouldn't have come.

Cherry   Don't get at me.

Paul   It was your bright idea.

Cherry   You're joking. I didn't want to trail all the way up here.

Paul   I told you, didn't I, like a nut-house. She'll only be crying for the next seven hours.

Cherry   I think she's just over-emotional.

Paul   You can say that agen. God ... Philip Larkin was right, you know. But I can't desert 'em. They need support from us.

Cherry   Hey come on, cheer up ... Have you got clean underpants on?

Paul   No ...

Cherry   Well ... I'm going to tell your mother.

Paul   You would and all.

Harry *enters from the kitchen.*

Harry   Sorry about that, kid; your mother's up and down all the time at the minute. You know what she's like. She says, she's not going out and I think she means it ... Sorry.

Silence.

Paul   Let me have a word wi her?

Harry   Come on, Cherry, let's me and you go and get some fresh air in the garden. I'll show you what a pit used to look like.

Harry *and* **Cherry** *leave.*

Paul (*calling*)   Mam ... ? Mother ... ?

Paul *exits.*

Music: 'I'll Be With You In Apple Blossom Time'. The lights fade.

Annie *slowly enters, and sits right. She sits alone for a moment, then* **May** *enters. It is later the same day.* **May** *is wearing a coat − she has simply thrown it on.*

Silence.

Annie   What do you want?

May   To see you.

Annie   Come for your records back?

May   No. Not really.

Annie   You can have 'em. There in a box int other room, cracked most of 'em.

May   Oh ... I got your card.

Annie   Can't afford a present. Card cost me ninety pence.

May   I thought I'd better come and see if you were still alive.

Annie   Been bad wi' me kidneys.

May   This house is a tip ... don't you clean it?

Annie   No, I don't bother. I sit here in the dark waiting to die.

May   I'll come and clean it for you.

Annie   You've no need.

May   Our Paul's come home, brought this Cherry.

Annie   Oh ay?

May   She looks nice. Likes me house.

Annie   That's nice for you.

May   He's taking me out to a carvery for me birthday.

Annie   Well, what you come here for?

May   Do you want to come?

Annie   I've got nowt to wear.

May   He says come as you are – I've just thrown me coat on. Are you coming or not?

Silence for as long as it will hold.

Annie   Well, I right fancy a dance.

May   Well bloody come on then.

Annie *exits at speed.*

Music: 'Black Seam' by Sting.

Harry, **Tosh**, **Paul** *and* **Cherry** *enter slowly.* **Annie** *returns, wearing a coat.*

Annie *looks to* **Paul**. *The lights shine on* **Paul** *from below, which gives the impression of a shaft of light on a coal seam and, effectively, cuts the stage in two. Slowly,* **Annie** *looks at the audience, and, as she does, all the cast begin to dance a modern dance slowly which gives a sinister effect.* **Paul** *envelops both his mother and his aunty, the three of them forming a picture, and* **Paul** *leads them in a bow.*

Curtain.

Methuen Contemporary Dramatists
include

Peter Barnes (three volumes)
Sebastian Barry
Dermot Bolger
Edward Bond (six volumes)
Howard Brenton
  (two volumes)
Richard Cameron
Jim Cartwright
Caryl Churchill (two volumes)
Sarah Daniels (two volumes)
Nick Darke
David Edgar (three volumes)
Ben Elton
Dario Fo (two volumes)
Michael Frayn (three volumes)
John Godber (two volumes)
Paul Godfrey
John Guare
Peter Handke
Jonathan Harvey
Declan Hughes
Terry Johnson (two volumes)
Sarah Kane
Bernard-Marie Koltès
David Lan
Bryony Lavery
Deborah Levy
Doug Lucie

David Mamet (three volumes)
Martin McDonagh
Duncan McLean
Anthony Minghella
  (two volumes)
Tom Murphy (four volumes)
Phyllis Nagy
Anthony Nielsen
Philip Osment
Louise Page
Stewart Parker (two volumes)
Joe Penhall
Stephen Poliakoff
  (three volumes)
Christina Reid
Philip Ridley
Willy Russell
Ntozake Shange
Sam Shepard (two volumes)
Wole Soyinka (two volumes)
David Storey (three volumes)
Sue Townsend
Michel Vinaver (two volumes)
Arnold Wesker (two volumes)
Michael Wilcox
David Wood (two volumes)
Victoria Wood

Methuen World Classics
include

Jean Anouilh (two volumes)
John Arden (two volumes)
Arden & D'Arcy
Brendan Behan
Aphra Behn
Bertolt Brecht (seven volumes)
Büchner
Bulgakov
Calderón
Čapek
Anton Chekhov
Noël Coward (eight volumes)
Eduardo De Filippo
Max Frisch
John Galsworthy
Gogol
Gorky
Harley Granville Barker
  (two volumes)
Henrik Ibsen (six volumes)
Lorca (three volumes)

Marivaux
Mustapha Matura
David Mercer (two volumes)
Arthur Miller (five volumes)
Molière
Musset
Peter Nichols (two volumes)
Clifford Odets
Joe Orton
A. W. Pinero
Luigi Pirandello
Terence Rattigan
  (two volumes)
W. Somerset Maugham
  (two volumes)
August Strindberg
  (three volumes)
J. M. Synge
Ramón del Valle-Inclán
Frank Wedekind
Oscar Wilde

Methuen Modern Plays
include work by

Jean Anouilh
John Arden
Margaretta D'Arcy
Peter Barnes
Sebastian Barry
Brendan Behan
Dermot Bolger
Edward Bond
Bertolt Brecht
Howard Brenton
Anthony Burgess
Simon Burke
Jim Cartwright
Caryl Churchill
Noël Coward
Lucinda Coxon
Sarah Daniels
Nick Darke
Nick Dear
Shelagh Delaney
David Edgar
David Eldridge
Dario Fo
Michael Frayn
John Godber
Paul Godfrey
David Greig
John Guare
Peter Handke
David Harrower
Jonathan Harvey
Iain Heggie
Declan Hughes
Terry Johnson
Sarah Kane
Charlotte Keatley
Barrie Keeffe
Howard Korder

Robert Lepage
Stephen Lowe
Doug Lucie
Martin McDonagh
John McGrath
Terrence McNally
David Mamet
Patrick Marber
Arthur Miller
Mtwa, Ngema & Simon
Tom Murphy
Phyllis Nagy
Peter Nichols
Joseph O'Connor
Joe Orton
Louise Page
Joe Penhall
Luigi Pirandello
Stephen Poliakoff
Franca Rame
Mark Ravenhill
Philip Ridley
Reginald Rose
David Rudkin
Willy Russell
Jean-Paul Sartre
Sam Shepard
Wole Soyinka
Shelagh Stephenson
C. P. Taylor
Theatre de Complicite
Theatre Workshop
Sue Townsend
Judy Upton
Timberlake Wertenbaker
Roy Williams
Victoria Wood

Methuen Student Editions

Jean Anouilh	*Antigone*
John Arden	*Serjeant Musgrave's Dance*
Alan Ayckbourn	*Confusions*
Aphra Behn	*The Rover*
Edward Bond	*Lear*
Bertolt Brecht	*The Caucasian Chalk Circle*
	Life of Galileo
	Mother Courage and her Children
Anton Chekhov	*The Cherry Orchard*
Caryl Churchill	*Top Girls*
Shelagh Delaney	*A Taste of Honey*
John Galsworthy	*Strife*
Robet Holman	*Across Oka*
Henrik Ibsen	*A Doll's House*
Charlotte Keatley	*My Mother Said I Never Should*
Bernard Kops	*Dreams of Anne Frank*
Federico García Lorca	*Blood Wedding*
	The House of Bernarda Alba
	(bilingual edition)
John Marston	*The Malcontent*
Willy Russell	*Blood Brothers*
Wole Soyinka	*Death and the King's Horseman*
August Strindberg	*The Father*
J. M. Synge	*The Playboy of the Western World*
Oscar Wilde	*The Importance of Being Earnest*
Tennessee Williams	*A Streetcar Named Desire*
	The Glass Menagerie
Timberlake Wertenbaker	*Our Country's Good*

For a complete catalogue of Methuen Drama titles
write to:

Methuen Drama
215 Vauxhall Bridge Road
London SW1V 1EJ

or you can visit our website at:

www.methuen.co.uk